The Decalogue Decoded

Fr. Brian Mullady, O.P.

The Decalogue Decoded

What You Never Learned about the Ten Commandments

EWTN PUBLISHING, INC.
Irondale, Alabama

EWTN Publishing, Inc.
5817 Old Leeds Road, Irondale, AL 35210

Distributed by Sophia Institute Press, Box 5284, Manchester, NH 03108.

Library of Congress Cataloging-in-Publication Data

Names: Mullady, Brian Thomas, author.
Title: The Decalogue decoded : what you never learned about the Ten commandments / Fr. Brian Mullady, O.P.
Description: Irondale : EWTN Publishing, Inc., 2019. | Includes bibliographical references.
Identifiers: LCCN 2019022866 | ISBN 9781682781036 (paperback)
Subjects: LCSH: Ten commandments. | Catholic Church—Doctrines.
Classification: LCC BV4655 .M828 2019 | DDC 222/.1606—dc23 LC record available at https://lccn.loc.gov/2019022866

First printing

To Mother Angelica
and all those connected to EWTN,
with prayerful thanks

Contents

Introduction

Our Origin and Destiny

In the beginning God created the heavens and the earth.
The earth was without form and void, and darkness was upon
the face of the deep; and the Spirit of God was moving over
the face of the waters. (Gen. 1:1–2)

Who is in this beginning, when God made the heavens and
earth? "In the beginning was the Word, and the Word was with
God, and the Word was God" (John 1:1). And it is the Word who
teaches us, instructs us, and directs us in the correct order of creation. Corresponding to that order, then, is the dynamism of the
Holy Spirit "moving over the face of the waters." Both the order of
the Word and the dynamism of the Holy Spirit are meant to make
what He has created, by a union of love, like Him.

Now, the primary characteristic of God is that He is one. Therefore, all the various states of being and lower orders of creation are
meant to obey the power of God's Mind and Law. In this way, they
are in a proper relationship of order and love with Him, seeking
to become one. Consider even the stones, which by gravity seek
unity with the earth. This is their order; this is, in a sense, their
act of love. The plants take in the air and the nutrients of the
soil and water and sunlight, and from those they make, through

1

photosynthesis, a growing, living being. This is their order, their love. The animals take in their surroundings and, through their sense knowledge, offer a unified action—a single self and life—corresponding to their nature in order and, in their distinctive way, in love of their Creator. But there is only one being that God has made who can truly arrive at full unity with Him; man is the only being who is able to comprehend and thus to unify all the things of the world in his mind—in their fullness, without subtracting any part of their nature.

The soul of man reflects in a unique way the perfection of his Creator. Man has an intellect, and in this he reflects the Word. He has a will, and in this he reflects the Spirit. And in the unity of intellect and will in a spiritual soul, he reflects the Father. All the other parts of creation, in trying to attain unity with God, are like His footprints—they remind us of Him and direct us to Him, but they resemble Him extremely incompletely. Man, however, is made in the image of God, and the Law of human nature is that he who came forth directly from God must end directly in unity with God. He who is an image of the Blessed Trinity must end in unity with that Trinity. And so, God gave us the ability to participate in His own nature. Saint Peter says this directly in his Second Letter: "He has granted to us his precious and very great promises, that through these you may escape from the corruption that is in the world because of passion, and become partakers of the divine nature" (2 Pet. 1:4).

The source of our ability to partake of this nature and this unity is twofold. First, God elevates us to Him. This is something that we cannot hope to imagine or to merit ourselves. In Baptism, God enters into our soul with sanctifying grace, changing us interiorly and raising us to become partners with Him, to speak with Him, to walk and talk with Him as an intimate. Secondly, God has given us free will, by which we imitate God and thus can be unified with Him.

Introduction

Men are different from animals, therefore, in that they are called by God to participate in discovering and attaining the unity of their being in Him *as a partner with Him*. After Adam named the animals, God said to him: "You may freely eat of every tree of the garden; but of the tree of the knowledge of good and evil you shall not eat, for in the day that you eat of it you shall die" (Gen. 2:16–17). This was the first law, and it was given distinctly to the being who could choose. It was a simple law, but it called upon human beings to demonstrate the unity of love for God that they had been offered through grace by choosing to obey Him.

In this we see that obedience and love are perfect companions. Peace with God depended on both the grace by which He elevated us to Him and our cooperation in this divine friendship through obedience. Law and love, that is, are not in conflict. Rather, when they find their source and their end in God, they are perfect expressions of human freedom. We can see this in the state in which Adam was created: He had the fullness of grace, and his human choice was easily and spontaneously at the service of that grace in the state of original justice.

The First Sin

So, when God told Adam and Eve that they were not permitted to eat of the Tree of the Knowledge of Good and Evil, this was not to take away their choice. They knew (in theory) the difference between good and evil; otherwise, they could not have made a choice. The "knowledge of good and evil" meant that when they disobeyed the Law of God, when they showed a lack of love by a lack of obedience, they would *experience directly* what evil meant, what sin meant. This sin impaired their nature.

Law, therefore, is not an inhibition of freedom, but an expression of freedom. It directs our choices toward what is good and beautiful.

Sin, on the other hand, is an inhibition of freedom because it reduces human possibility to the puny point of view of man. More than that, sin takes away the marvelous integration God had given Adam and Eve in their original creation, a marvelous integration built on divine intimacy.

Adam's intellect in choice was freely and spontaneously at the disposal of God. He enjoyed continuously infused contemplation. His will experienced no direction to malice but was drawn only to giving the gift of love that he had received. His emotions supported his choices for good. In one of the psalms, we read, "My heart and flesh sing for joy to the living God" (84:2). This is the unity of the intellect, the will, and the emotions in choice. And Adam's body perfectly reflected that, because God preserved his body from all suffering and death.

Regardless of what the civil order does, regardless of how our technology advances, it's not possible for us to live a fully human life without the direction of the Law of God. It's not possible for us to overcome ignorance, malice, weakness, and death without the direction of the Law of God. Just because we can make better toilets and put a man on the moon does not mean that we have the answer for the alienation of the human heart that was caused by Original Sin.

Original Sin leads to rebellion and sickness in the human race. It does not mean, as some mistaken theologies teach, that we are now totally depraved. We can still do good acts. We each still have an intellect, a will, emotions, and a body, all good because they were created by God—but what we cannot do is get it all finally together. The Greek philosophers recognized this. Aristotle, after examining the beauty and depth the human character is capable of, ends by saying that he does not actually know anyone like that. The Greeks experienced the tragedy of human existence for centuries, as did all the other pagans. They knew there was something wrong, but they did not know that what was wrong was a loss of the interior integrity of the gift of grace. The Jews experienced the same thing. Even after they had received the Law, they continued to wander into idolatry and to fall away because they did not have grace. The human race needed redemption.

The Law Kills — and Heals

Revealed law is found in the Ten Commandments and in the Sermon on the Mount. So, if we're going to discuss the Ten Commandments, it's essential to recognize that the Law of God — His truth and His order — is necessary for the direction and the perfection of our freedom. The two aspects of freedom that distinguish man from the animals and conform him to the image of God are the intellect and the will. And it is in the intellect and the will that God allows the human race to suffer the punishments of Original Sin in the deepest way. For centuries, the human race wandered in the blindness of mind and the weakness of will that characterized the punishments of Original Sin. In the Law given on Mount Sinai, Moses initiated the cure for this. God, through Moses, revealed to us what human nature could and should be like.

Now, human beings could have discovered much of this law on their own, but the fullness of the idea that the unity of human character had to be the same unity as that found in the Trinity was not clear. On Mount Sinai, God enlightened the mind with the remedy for the blindness of ignorance. In these Ten Commandments, God sought to teach us what Adam and Eve had known before the Fall without even having to think about it — the truth about our nature that has not changed and will not change through the centuries. These Ten Commandments, by revealing to us what our nature demands and entails, are the beginning of God's progressive cure for the ills of the human race.

The trouble was that the Law did not by itself give the grace of the Spirit back to man. This is why we are told that the Law kills (2 Cor. 3:6). It's not that the Ten Commandments are the cause of death, but that they are the occasion of death. They multiply sin because the person who has been instructed in them has no more excuse for not knowing that all the actions of the body, all the movements of the emotions, and all the desires of the will and the intellect have to be ordered back to God. And for this integrity to be achieved, the Spirit of Grace is necessary.

God did this in preparation for His Son, in whom the Law would be fulfilled. Before Christ, the prophets testified to the true meaning of the Law, which reflects a human character that is completed in a mystical marriage with God, as were Adam's and Eve's. In other words, the occasions of sinning that became more frequent and upsetting when they had the Law but did not look to the Messiah made the Jews realize their own weakness and their need for Him.

The end of all the Commandments is the union of God in the soul, which is the virtue of charity, or love of God. Nothing we do can finally lead to this integration without charity. Even the charismatic gifts of the Holy Spirit have no final force for us — though they may be of use to others — without charity.

> If I speak in the tongues of men and of angels, but have not love, I am a noisy gong or a clanging cymbal. And if I have prophetic powers, and understand all mysteries and all knowledge, and if I have all faith, so as to remove mountains, but have not love, I am nothing. If I give away all I have, and if I deliver my body to be burned, but have not love, I gain nothing. (1 Cor. 13:1–3)

The Law began the progressive cure of the human race by pointing out to men that they were created in and made for the Trinity — that is, that their intellect, will, and choosing faculties were made in the image of the Trinity and that they could discover the unity of character again only through the Trinity. It is necessary, then, for those who practice the Law to realize that it is ordered to and completed by love. Therefore, the Law is perfectly fulfilled in Christ. As we said earlier, it is through the ordering Word of God that the Spirit entices us to live.

And then Jesus tells us the true meaning of the Law. In fact, Mount Sinai finds its perfect companion in the Sermon on the Mount, where Jesus does away with the reduction of the Law to legalistic interpretations. Perhaps most famously, He taught: "You have heard that it was said, 'You shall not commit adultery.' But I say to you that every one who looks at a woman lustfully has already committed adultery with her in his heart" (Matt. 5:27–28). And concerning avoiding anger and retaliation and embracing love, He used that same formula: "You have heard it said ... but I say to you ..." He Who is the embodiment of wisdom shows us what these Ten Commandments really and finally mean for us: They fulfill the Beatitudes and are fulfilled in the virtues.

Modern Confusions

There are a couple of modern difficulties—dating most clearly from the eighteenth century—that have made understanding the Commandments especially difficult for us. First, the English philosopher David Hume argued that we could come to know anything only from information gathered from the five senses. Therefore, there was no way to describe any non-concrete realities—such as ethics and morality and the meaning of life itself—except through our feelings. Hume defined what is good, then, as what felt good to the greatest number. On this understanding, though, the idea of a universal or natural law becomes unintelligible. We are left to wonder: Is the Law just my projection of my feelings about what should be right and wrong onto the whole human race? On a Humean understanding, there can be no objectivity in morality.

Then the German philosopher Immanuel Kant completed the pincer. He recognized that something wasn't quite right in Hume: There had to be, Kant realized, a right and wrong that everybody could know and describe. But the trouble was that he accepted Hume's presupposition that we can't describe these notions of right and wrong because we can't arrive at them through our senses. His solution was to assert that the Law must come to us as something we know innately, without any investigation into the world whatsoever.

These two views lead to a destructive divorce among the basic experiences we have in our souls: feelings and sense experiences, on the one hand, and reason and, consequently, law on the other. Hume emphasized only the feelings; this has come down to us in the form of the perverse ethic "If it feels good, do it." Or with Kant, we might affirm that only reason — that innate sense by which we can discern right and wrong — matters, but this reason is totally separate from growing in the emotional or spiritual life.

This is not the Christian way of looking at the Law, nor was it the Jewish way. The Law is neither a subjective collection of irrational preferences that we project onto everybody else, nor a coldly rational and abstract collection of assertions made without reference to genuine human experience. In other words, this divorce of sense and emotion from reason leads us either to sacrifice the individual to Law or the Law to the individual — pure feeling and individuality as opposed to duty, or pure duty as opposed to feeling and individuality. This is expressed neither by the Ten Commandments nor by the interpretation of them that Christ gives on the Sermon on the Mount.

The duty imposed by Law is neither arbitrary nor strictly abstract: It is an expression of the deep truth of human and divine nature. It is an expression of the power of the soul to integrate the complete self: the body, because the terms of the Law are generally expressed using the body; the emotions, because they must be virtuously attuned and spontaneously reactive to the rule of Law; and the reason, because the Law is understood by the intellect. All of these things combine beautifully and perfectly to motivate, stimulate, and support the union of our wills in love with the true reality of the world.

This integration is open to everybody. The Jews were given its fullest expression in the Ten Commandments, but it was even open to the Gentiles. "When Gentiles who have not the law do by nature what the law requires, they are a law to themselves, even though they do not have the law" (Rom. 2:14). All the moral precepts of the Law are meant to reflect the truths revealed to us not only by God directly, but also by nature. They're meant to teach us how nature expresses itself and realizes itself.

Now, some people think that this talk about "nature" reduces man to the level of the animals—the "natural" world of instinct. By "nature," however, we mean how man carries out actions to fulfill the purpose or "end" given to us by God: eternal union with Him. In some cases, we may have things in common with animals, such as the simple necessity and instinct to eat nutritious food. But our nature is also fulfilled through distinctly human qualities, such as love and choice directed to our destiny with God. The Commandments, then, inasmuch as they address our nature, can be known at least in their basics by everyone—certainly the ones that have to do with theft and murder and adultery.

The Tablets

When God gave Moses the Ten Commandments, He did so on two tablets. This division was meaningful, separating the laws based

The Decalogue Decoded

on their object—God or our fellow men. The first three commandments, having to do specifically with love of God, lay the foundation for the rest and were on that first tablet.

The second tablet had to do with our relationship with our neighbors. These commandments are about not just actions but the interior disposition of love with which our actions are to be performed. God gave these tablets to Moses to instruct us in what a human being who is filled with the unity of His Presence should act like—the interior integration that is expressed through exterior actions.

All these Commandments, as we've said, were given to us as a preparation for the Word of God Himself, Who is the Truth, to take flesh to redeem us. We can distinguish two basic ways in which the Commandments were intended to prepare us, based on the two tablets. First, relating to the first tablet, it was necessary for us to believe in His Father. How could we accept the Son Who would redeem us if we did not believe in His Father? The cornerstone of the Ten Commandments, then, must be monotheism. The second tablet, then, prepared the people for Christ by encouraging them to leave behind their habits that contradicted the image of God present within them. The last seven commandments, that is, were meant to move the people away from sin through knowledge of what is and is not in accord with growing in relationship with our Creator. This would work in two ways: in a positive way, through the force of the Commandments themselves, and in a negative way, by showing them what their lives were like without a Redeemer.

Now, every part of the Law has to do with the notion of community. Indeed, when God gave the Commandments on Mount Sinai, He wished to establish a community—not a civil community but a divine community in which He was the head. The Law recognizes a common good that is fulfilled by a return to unity with the Creator. The community of Israel, therefore, was the beginning

10

of what we know as the Church, which is the commonwealth of God and the fulfillment of the natural law.

In every community, it's necessary that the relationship between the ruler and the members of the community and the relationships among the members be well ordered. Thus, in the first three commandments we find laws pertaining to the first relationship, ours with God. In the other seven commandments — called the juridical precepts — we see how to treat our fellow men right.

Beginning with our duties to God, the very first one is fidelity. If we are to be united in all our powers and character with the Blessed Trinity, we have to acknowledge the primacy and unity and eternity of the Blessed Trinity. This, fundamentally, is the First Commandment. Part of acknowledging this primacy, of course, is to show reverence by doing nothing to injure His Supreme Goodness or Truth by disrespecting His Name — the Second Commandment. And then, integrity of mind, will, heart, and strength demands that we show Him service. This is expressed in the Third Commandment, that we serve Him in a special way on the Sabbath.

The first tablet of the law is primarily figurative and not literal. It prepares us for the heavenly Sabbath and the heavenly liturgy. Since it commands love of God, the letter of the law must not be so emphasized that the spirit is destroyed. Christ talked about this in the famous: "The sabbath was made for man, not man for the sabbath" (Mark 2:27). He emphasized the cleaning of the soul as the meaning of the symbolic ritual cleansing of vessels.

Then the Commandments turn to our duties with respect to the members of the commonwealth of God — that is, anyone who is made in His image. First, in the Fourth Commandment, we see how once we have acknowledged God in fidelity, in reverence, and in service, we must show honor and piety to those who, in a special way, take His place in our lives: parents, pastors, friends, one's country. The next four commandments, then, address deeds done with the body against the images of God who form our community: destroying the substance of another human being through murder; destroying the most intimate of human relationships, which image the Divine Holy Trinity, through adultery; or destroying social trust and others' sustenance and reputation through theft or slander. Finally, not only are deeds and words addressed in the Commandments, but even the very desires that motivate them. And so, the final two commandments forbid us not only to take but to covet — to cultivate a disordered love toward things or other persons. The second tablet of the law is to be interpreted as emphasizing the literal over the figurative. One must literally not cheat others, must tell the truth, and must respect parents, the right to life, and marriage.

The spiritual meaning of the Law, which emphasizes both love of God and love of neighbor, is examined and promoted in the prophets. Their teachings are necessary to proclaim and live the law properly. The wisdom literature in which the virtues are extolled also must be referenced. The *Catechism of the Catholic Church* (CCC) quotes Wisdom 8:7: "If anyone loves righteousness, [Wisdom's] labors are virtues; for she teaches temperance and prudence, justice and courage" (1805). The *Catechism* further points out: 'The goal of the virtuous life is to become like God" (1803).[1]

All the Commandments, then, have to do with the virtues, letting our exterior actions be ordered by the interior integrity of the soul, which is to be ordered toward God, in Whom it is created and toward Whom it is directed. As the psalm says:

> The law of the LORD is perfect,
>   reviving the soul;
> the testimony of the LORD is sure,
>   making wise the simple;

---

[1] Quoting Saint Gregory of Nyssa, *De beatitudinibus*, 1.

the precepts of the LORD are right,
 rejoicing the heart;
the commandment of the LORD is pure,
 enlightening the eyes;
the fear of the LORD is clean,
 enduring for ever;
the ordinances of the LORD are true,
 and righteous altogether. (19:7–9)

For the rest of this book we will discuss each of the Command-ments in order. We will see what a divine gift they are to us, why we have to believe in them, why we have to meditate upon them, and why we have to examine our consciences accordingly. They all point us toward virtues — virtues that must flow from wills that are filled with God.

The First Commandment

A Firm Foundation

The First Commandment is the foundation stone of the community of Israel, and indeed of man himself: "I am the LORD your God.... You shall have no other gods before me" (Exod. 20:2–3). This, right here, is where our deepest identity and deepest dignity are found.

The Commandments, though generally framed in terms of prohibitions, are really about this: our dignity and the relationship of love that God offers us. The First Commandment, especially, is an expression of a kind of marital love God shares with us. We have the dignity of being called to an exclusive, personal, loving, intimate relationship with Him Who transcends the world! Therefore, we are called to a dignity that transcends ourselves and, indeed, everything this world has to offer. And so, when we break one of the Commandments, we deny our dignity. The Commandments are meant to teach us this dignity and how to honor it; here, we see how the First Commandment lays this foundation.

Indeed, this is the most basic, the bedrock of all the Commandments. It shows us that, just as in every spousal relationship on earth, fidelity is necessary; without it, no other aspects of the relationship can form and thrive. Our fidelity to God guarantees our dignity as being made in His image. The First Commandment (and all the others, for that matter) is not just a suggestion, a recommendation, a helpful hint. The modern tendency is to see no moral laws as truly obligatory, but if we misstep here, we can't get any further along in the journey to holiness and, ultimately, to communion with God. And that is where our dignity lies: in our innate capability to be a partner in the divine nature.

Now, we must remember that only the interior presence of the Holy Spirit can lead to the perfect observance of this commandment. The Law can cure our ignorance and teach us what was right. But, little by little, through His grace and His spirit, God must also cure our malice by restoring His interior presence. This commandment, then, calls us to recognize in all our actions that there is a God, that that God is One, and that we are called to Him in spousal Love. This acknowledgment of the One God is the essential foundation for the full realization of the potential of the human soul. This is how we prepare ourselves for our destined union with God, by exercising an interior virtue that orients our actions toward Him, that acknowledges Him to be the primary source of everything good, and that worships Him in a manner that is fitting to Him.

The Virtue of Religion

This virtue, by which we render to God what is due to Him, is classically called the virtue of religion. Now, ancient philosophers such as Aristotle argued that virtues were the mean, or average, between an excess and a defect. The mean is not mediocrity! Remember God's words in Revelation 3:16: "So, because you are lukewarm, and neither cold nor hot, I will spew you out of my mouth." Rather, the mean of a virtue is a judgment of proportionality, of what is fitting and proper. What is the kind of relationship with God that is suited to our souls, that is proper for a created being like us? This is determined by the reality of Who He is, and He is infinitely greater and more powerful and more living than we are! He is not even a part of the created universe — and yet He gives being and movement and life to everything in the universe — including us. And so, we must recognize this fact by returning to Him in true and authentic worship. That is the mean: the only kind of relationship fitting for a created being to his all-powerful, all-loving Creator.

When we devote ourselves to someone or something as we would to God, we fail to recognize the truth that the final goodness of the human race can be fulfilled only in Someone Who is at once distinct from and intimately involved with the created world. This is a denial of our divine destiny in that it denies both His heavenly separateness from us and the possibility of union with Him, now and, after death, forever. This is the unity to which our souls are called by this commandment.

The virtue of religion is a part of the virtue of justice, which is the constant and perpetual will to render to another his due. The flip side of a duty is a right. One becomes a subject of a right either by nature or by a human institution, such as civil law. God is a subject of rights because He is the Creator Who gives us everything, up to and including life, truth, and goodness themselves. Every man, then, has a duty to recognize the rights of God, and therefore our duties to Him, as Someone who can never be repaid for these gifts. The virtue of religion is the attempt by man to fulfill his duties to God in justice.

This is not the same as charity, which is the union of our hearts with the Creator. Rather, it involves a movement of both body and soul to recognize and seek to repay God, to do justice to Him. These virtues are related but are not the same. The first three commandments address potential defects in this most basic of human duties and tell us what their proper expression looks like.

The Decalogue Decoded

The First Commandment proscribes excesses of religion and the Second Commandment defects in religion, while the Third commands the acts that form the necessary foundation of the virtue of religion as an obligation in justice on the whole human race. Aristotle recognized that the virtue of justice was limited if it was interpreted merely as a calculated quid pro quo or a recognition of rights among equals.

Speaking of an excess in religion raises the question: How can we possibly worship God in excess? Here, though, "excess" doesn't mean "too much," but "in a disordered way." And so, we run afoul of the First Commandment and commit an excess of religion if we give devotion in a manner that is not fitting to God, or if we worship someone or something that is not God. This is the vice of superstition, which is expressed in three ways. The first is idolatry, which is worshipping part of the created world. The second is divinization, which involves making pacts with demons to obtain knowledge of things that no one has a right to know—and that the demons themselves never even know. The third is superstitious observances, which have to do with using objects such as amulets, charms, and crystals as though they had the power to bind God.

Authentic versus Counterfeit Religion

We can worship God in an undo manner in several ways. First, there is syncretism, in which rites and rituals from other religious traditions are imported into or mixed with Catholic traditions. This was a problem in the early Church: Saint Paul, for instance, admonished those who tried to return to an older expression of religion, such as continuing to regard circumcision as a spiritual necessity, when they had been given the New Covenant in Jesus Christ. There were other forms of pre-Christian worship that, not imbued with the Holy Spirit, amounted to worshipped matter—which means, in practice, worshipping demons. Since the coming of Christ, though, there is no other valid form of worship but His, exemplified and culminated in the fullness of His Sacrifice upon the Cross. This once-and-for-all Sacrifice, made present at every Mass, is now the only valid expression of our fidelity to the one God, and thus of the virtue of religion.

Some well-meaning people would like to use in Catholic spirituality, as an aid to evangelization, elements from other cultures that have been less influenced by the Church through the ages. When done well—and it can be done very well!—this is called inculturation. While there are, however, strictly speaking, true elements in every religious tradition, there are also some elements, especially of worship, that simply cannot be introduced into the Church without also denying key truths about Christ and His Sacrifice.

For instance, some have brought Native American and other indigenous religious rituals, such as dances, into the Mass. Purely as a kind of art, this might be just aesthetically or liturgically unappealing, but the problem goes deeper: These rituals are often, by their nature, invocations of pagan spirits or deities, which might well be demons. There is no way to bring these into Catholic worship without transgressing the virtue of religion and violating the First Commandment.

There are also Eastern practices of prayer that focus on "centering" or "emptying" oneself. These practices, many people tell me, lead them to the experience of peace. But I would suggest that this sensation is more like that induced by a drug trance. It's true that continuous measured breathing can have the result of leading a person to a kind of altered consciousness. But this is not the same as the peace induced by God in His authentic Sacrifice. The center and the focus of authentic prayer is God, not the self. Certain practicing of "emptying" may bear a superficial resemblance to the prayer of quiet. However, the authentic prayer of quiet is not induced by us or our wills; this kind of prayer is a gift granted by God to those who are already prepared for it by the active life.

On the opposite end of the noise spectrum, some charismatics maintain that they can employ the gift of tongues during Mass for a certain period of time. This cannot be the gift of tongues, though, as we do not control the time or place when charisms are given; only God can do that. This could be a kind of spontaneous praise, but it is definitely not the gift of tongues described in the Bible.

Knowing Our Place

Another way worship can be disordered is through the usurping of the proper roles of ordained ministers. For example, preaching homilies at Mass is, according to the *Code of Canon Law*, restricted to ordained bishops, priests, and deacons. If someone wants to make a special announcement on the parish finances or to discuss enrollment in the parish school, that's fine. But it is forbidden for laypeople to make a commentary on Holy Scripture at the time of the homily. We even find occasions of "dialogue homilies," in which various people take their parts in explaining Scripture. This is unfitting worship of God.

Well-meaning people have sometimes sought to force changes in the Church by declaring themselves ordained to a certain ritual part in the Mass without being ordained by a lawfully designated bishop. There are examples of religious sisters claiming they are deacons, wearing diaconal vestments, and exercising roles that are reserved to a deacon at Mass. This is also condemned by the First Commandment. A theory of ordination taught in the 1970s claimed that the Rite of Ordination did not make one a priest or a deacon, but that it was only a kind of public affirmation of an interior process that had already taken place. Some taught that women were priests or deacons if they thought they were. This is superstition.

Idols Everywhere

We can also sin against the First Commandment and, therefore, against religion through the objects of our worship—that is, through idolatry. This is the sin that is fundamental to materialism and paganism. In idolatry, undue worship is given to a created thing or a person.

In the ancient world, people could, in a sense, be excused for this sin due to their ignorance. When the first philosophers ruminated over reasonable explanations for the existence of the world, they were filled with enthusiasm and wonder. What these earliest thinkers, though, could not yet understand was that the Creator was not part of our created world but was a Spirit. (Socrates and the later Greek philosophers discovered this without looking for it, but they could not get to the full truth without divine revelation.) Only having matter before them, they tended to identify their version of god with matter. And so they worshipped fire, earth, air, or water—what they considered to be the primary elements that made up creation.

The ancients would also sometimes worship their fellow men, especially their leaders, as gods. Lawgivers and emperors were declared to be divine. This was due in part to the recognized difficulty of making good laws, and in part to a straightforward exaltation of a human being due to the power of governance. This error, though, was not limited to the past; it returned with a vengeance in the twentieth century with the veneration of totalitarian leaders and regimes. When true religion seems to have passed away, the state suddenly looks like a good candidate for worship. But there is only one universal order worthy of our veneration, and that is Holy Mother Church.

The Decalogue Decoded

Now, some people have regarded depictions of Christ and the saints as idolatry, but this is, frankly, nonsense. The "graven images" spoken of in Scripture are not at all the same as the statues, icons, or other art we use in church. After all, the Israelites themselves were commanded by God to make some images, such as the cherubim that covered the Mercy Seat in the Ark of the Covenant, or the serpent on a pole (see Exod. 25:10–22; Num. 21:4–9). In addition to this, in the New Testament, since Christ has come in a human body there is now a whole new "economy" of images (see CCC 2131).

We place these representations in our churches for the same reason that we place images of great men in public places—not to revere the stone of which they're made, but as occasions to honor them and to contemplate their virtues. The Seventh Council of Nicaea in 787 approved this practice against the iconoclasts. The theological explanation is clearly taught in Thomas Aquinas and expressed in the *Catechism of the Catholic Church*: "The movement toward the image does not terminate in it as image, but tends toward that whose image it is" (2132).[2] Sacred artworks are not objects of worship but are occasions of worship and invitations to prayer. How sad it is to walk into a church where the crucifixes have been stripped and the icons removed and the frescoes whitewashed out of some misguided fear of opulence or idolatry! We might as well take all the pictures of our families out of our homes because they somehow violate our love for our families.

We might also commit idolatry by choosing to organize our lives around some earthly good—money or power or pleasure—rather than union with the God Who made us. This is even a kind of paganism, elevating earthly goods to the status of divinity. Make no mistake about it: All idolatry is a sin. We cannot make idols of celebrities, of rulers, of ancestors, of artists, of athletes—of anyone.

[2] Quoting Saint Thomas Aquinas, *Summa Theologiae*, II-II, 81, 3, ad. 3.

Even if these people may represent some kind of divine gift to us, we cannot substitute the gift for the giver.

There is another kind of idolatry or superstition that emerges from disordered curiosity—the desire to know that which can't or shouldn't be known. This is divinization. There are so many examples: the future, the thoughts of others, and so on. Now, of course, natural phenomena such as the rising of the sun or the progress of a disease are predictable by genuine science. But to access other, contingent information known only to God—How long will I live? Who will I marry? Which horse will win the race?—we might be tempted to invoke other spiritual sources.

Let's be clear: Any divination of spirits will always invoke the antagonists in the supernatural realm—the demons, not the angels who are obedient to God. The existence of demons is defined doctrine in the Church. The devil is real, and he hates God and he hates you; he and his cohort of fallen angels are looking for any way to get at us and take us away from God. Sometimes these demons represent themselves—through occult means such as tarot cards or Ouija boards or even "playful" things such as astrology—as knowing something that they do not and cannot know. But in so doing, they invite us to give ourselves over to them, jeopardizing our souls.

Superstition Is Not Harmless

The final form of irreligion is superstitious observances: trying to use aspects of God's created world—talismans, charms, crystals—to influence Him or wrest control away from Him and for ourselves. It does not matter if you think you're doing this kind of thing for a good reason or a good end: It's still an attempt to manipulate the world by material forces! Witchcraft is based on the idea that one can take power from nature; use it for a human purpose, good or ill; and then return that power to nature. This involves turning

"Mother Nature" into a divinity, which is a sin shared by druidry. Sadly, druidry and witchcraft are becoming all too common again. In the past, accusations of witchcraft were sometimes used against people, especially women, who simply used natural modes of healing or who were somehow social inconveniences—but this should not lead us to underestimate the extent of real witchcraft.

One further point is important. What about magic? What is normally practiced in magic shows does not violate the First Commandment. Sleight-of-hand tricks and so forth have no moral meaning one way or the other. There is a kind of magic, however, that uses rituals in an attempt to bind God to act in a certain way, and this is contrary to this commandment.

It is important, also, that we think of the genuine sacramentals of the Church—rosaries and holy water and medals and so forth—not as possessing some magic influence over God or the world around us ("good luck charms"), but as aids to our relationship and unity with Him. In all the objects we use for our worship, we must remember the primacy of God and the fulfillment of Christ's Sacrifice. This way, we demonstrate rather than violate the fidelity we owe Him.

Foundation of Fidelity

And so the First Commandment functions in two ways. First, positively, God is seeking to recall a lost love—that is, us—to Himself. He wants us to return to the true marriage for which our souls were created. And as we've said, this relationship demands fidelity. The cornerstone and natural foundation of this love is the recognition and acknowledgment of the true God in the worship that is commanded by the law of nature and the virtue of religion. And second, negatively, the commandment is meant to prohibit those acts or other movements of the will that deny the reality of God's primacy.

This is the most basic, foundational duty that human beings owe to God. In our exterior practices, we must acknowledge the primacy of the God Who is both distinctive in His divinity and most intimate with us, and we do this by offering Him the deepest, most important devotion our human nature can offer—worship. Thus, we acknowledge the marriage of heaven and earth in our souls, made in His image.

The Second Commandment

Divine Respect

The Second Commandment continues the work of the First, inviting us back into a loving union with God by extending the teaching about fidelity to the very name of God Himself. Whereas the First Commandment addresses what were classically called excesses with respect to the virtue of religion, the Second addresses defects of that, which fall under the category of the vice of irreligion. Now that we've acknowledged God in fidelity, we are called upon not to hold Him in contempt in the way we treat His Name and His truth in our everyday lives: "You shall not take the name of the LORD your God in vain" (Exod. 20:7).

It's important to make distinctions all the time, but especially here at the beginning of this discussion. What is the specific difference between taking God's Name vainly and using it justly? The key point is this: When a person takes God's Name in vain, he fails to show proper reverence to God's nature by using Him to witness to something that is untrue or to affirm something that is evil.

As for taking God's Name justly, first we can use His name to confirm the truth, as in taking an oath in court. We can also use God's Name for our own sanctification, such as when we invoke the name of the Trinity in the Glory Be, or in praise, as we do in Mass (think of the Gloria) or in song. We can take vows, such as those to join a religious order or to complete some other good work, provided it's something proper and possible to complete. And sometimes we can even invoke God's Name to help us to admonish or to expel a demon—though genuine exorcisms must be reserved for the proper ministers. In none of these ways does one take the Name of the Lord in vain because he does not call upon God to witness to a falsity or to aid in an evil act. Rather, these applications of His Name affirm that God is Truth itself.

I Swear to God

The sin of perjury is lying under oath, especially in court. A perjurer calls on God to witness solemnly to a statement one knows to be false. We're not used to thinking of oaths as being genuinely binding—and as genuinely invoking God. We hear the words on television all the time, but they've become meaningless. But when we swear to God that we are telling the truth, that really does make a difference! And to ignore or to violate such an oath is an act of deep irreverence to God. It invokes Him Who is Truth itself in service of a lie, thus *compounding* the lie with an injury against God. Just as asking a friend to attest to something that is untrue damages that relationship, implicating God in deceit damages our relationship with Him.

Perjury is also, of course, an injury to others—specifically, a sin against the justice due to them in the form of their good name and the truth itself. We thus damage our own trustworthiness in the eyes of others, and the less men can trust one another's word, the less friendliness and peace there is in society.

Due to the seriousness of perjury, one should never lightly demand that another person take an oath—especially a known liar, whom it would be useless and vain to trust, and whom you would invite to commit grave sin. (Of course, judges and other public officials may demand such an oath from an untrustworthy person in their official capacity.) Oaths are serious business and, in private circumstances, should be offered or entered into only in very important matters.

Putting God to the Test

Besides the obvious example of perjury, there are other forms of irreligion that are forbidden by this commandment. The first is called tempting God. When Satan tempted Christ in the desert with food and power, He simply replied, "You shall not tempt the Lord your God" (Matt. 4:7). What does it mean to tempt or test God? It can mean demanding, whether out of ignorance or arrogance or faithlessness, that He demonstrate for us His power or His knowledge. It can also mean presumptuously relying on God's aid in something that we could readily do ourselves, such as tossing oneself off a cliff without a parachute or refusing medication while praying for God's intervention.

It's not uncommon, especially in the excitement of a recent conversion or another religious experience, to want or to expect everything to be a miracle. That is, sometimes we expect God to come through for us without doing anything ourselves. God wants to help us! But He most often works through us—through our prayerful and sometimes strenuous efforts to achieve good things for others and for ourselves. Too often, for instance, I hear about parents who pray fiercely for their adult children who are addicted to drugs—all while enabling them and covering for them so that their children never have to take responsibility.

Jesus ran into this attitude, as we see throughout the Gospels. When He promised the Samaritan woman His living water, she replied, "Sir, give me this water, that I may not thirst, nor come here to draw" (John 4:15). She wanted a miraculous supply that she wouldn't have to work for ever again. And then, of course, there were the loaves and the fishes. People began coming to Jesus because they wanted to make Him a bread king; He had given them food without their having to work for it—and they wanted it again and again.

Tempting God, then, involves doubt about God's nature—His knowledge and His power and His goodness. And puny man tries to set himself up as the judge of whether God lives up to His billing. How absurd: The creature desires to judge the strength and the truth and the power of the Creator!

In our post-Christian secular age, this is all too common. Years ago, C. S. Lewis wrote a book about it called *God in the Dock*, referring to the place in an English courtroom where the accused stands. Modern man, following Enlightenment philosophy, looks upon God as a creation Himself, a projection of human needs. The followers of Immanuel Kant, for instance, maintained that a religion without God was just as good as a religion with God, as long as we experience feelings of dependency on some higher power and are thereby led to be philanthropic toward others.

The ideal Kantian ecclesiastic, therefore, is a combination of a socialist and a socialite (with apologies to the British comedy series *Yes, Prime Minister*, which describes the ideal Church of England bishop this way). Nietzsche, relying on this account of things, said that if man created God, then for man to become truly himself, God must die. And so, people in contemporary Western society accuse God of causing all sorts of evils in the world. Their attitude is that God must prove Himself to them if they are to believe in Him.

Now, another important distinction: There are instances in Holy Scripture where people, including the Apostles, asked God to confirm something by means of signs. This is not the same as tempting God, because they asked out of faith that He could perform the sign, not out of doubt or suspicion. Their desire was to prove the truth of their words about the Faith to others, not to themselves. They also asked God to give support to their doctrine and their claims that they were indeed shepherds who participated in the mission of Christ the Good Shepherd. So, they were not faithless people seeking justifications for their lack of belief; rather, they were believers beseeching God to help them convert the world.

Despite the gravity of this sin of tempting God, we should note that it is not as bad as the sin of superstition, breaking the First Commandment. Superstition regards a lack of faith in God that is general and continuous, but tempting God is usually just one act of doubt.

Profaning the Sacred

Another vice against the Second Commandment is that of sacrilege, which refers to the violation or misuse of holy things. Objects or persons against whom sacrilege can be committed are those that are directly connected to the honor and worship that we owe to God and are meant to elevate us beyond the ordinary life of the senses: vestments, vessels, altars, other blessed items, and the bodies of priests themselves. It makes me want to cry to walk into a house and see religious articles being used merely as décor; in one house — a religious house! — I saw an altar that had been taken out of the church and was now being used as a table for a television set. He who dishonors that which is used for divine worship dishonors God. A former cathedral in a large city was sold, but the altar and the confessionals could not be removed. The altar was used as a bar when the former church was rented out for parties, and fallen-away Catholics used the confessionals to mock the sacrament of Penance.

Sacrilege can also occur with the abuse of sacred persons. To assault a priest or a bishop because he is a priest or a bishop is an attack on God, because these men, by virtue of their ordination, represent Him. Thus, the sin of sacrilege is added to the assault. (On the other hand, if a priest were to attack someone, the person would not be committing sacrilege in defending himself; his self-defense would be against the priest as an individual man, not because of his vocation.)

And then, of course, there is God Himself, fully present in the Blessed Sacrament. First of all, there is irreverence for Christ in the Sacrament in the form of carelessness in handling His Body and Blood. One hears, for instance, of the Precious Blood being poured down the sacrarium (which is reserved for cleaning the Communion vessels), rather than being consumed. I have seen particles of consecrated Hosts—sometimes prepared illicitly with leaven in the Western Church—thrown out as if they were nothing more than crumbs of ordinary bread. This is not just careless liturgical practice; it is sacrilege.

A recent Church document addressed this sad issue, which is caused by a lack of faith in the Eucharist:

> In accordance with what is laid down by the canons, "one who throws away the consecrated species or takes them away or keeps them for a sacrilegious purpose, incurs a latae sententiae [automatic] excommunication reserved to the Apostolic See; a cleric, moreover, may be punished by another penalty, not excluding dismissal from the clerical state." To be regarded as pertaining to this case is any action that is voluntarily and gravely disrespectful of the sacred species. Anyone, therefore, who acts contrary to these norms, for example casting the sacred species into the sacrarium or in an unworthy place or on the ground, incurs the penalties laid down.[3]

People can also commit sacrilege by receiving Christ unworthily. While we should not become too scrupulous about Confession, who

---

[3] Congregation of Divine Worship and the Discipline of the Sacraments, *Redemptionis Sacramentum* (March 25, 2004), no. 107.

could doubt that the problem today is quite the opposite: no under-standing at all that our mortal sins render us unworthy to receive Communion. To receive the Blessed Sacrament deliberately in a state of unworthiness is to commit a sacrilege. It is to present one-self for the Divine Gift without being interiorly prepared for Him.

Profane Profit

Another example of irreligion addressed in this commandment is the sin of simony, which is profaning the spiritual through the act of buying and selling. The name comes from Simon Magus in the Acts of the Apostles, who tried to buy from the Apostles the power to call down the Holy Spirit (Acts 8:18–24). Simply put, the spiritual cannot be reduced to material considerations, such as a price in money or other goods. There are obvious examples: the sale of indulgences, as was done in the Middle Ages, and markets in relics. One of the reasons the Church does not certify relics unless they are received from a specific agency in Rome is to cut down on spurious relics and trafficking in them.

The practice of having religious goods blessed only after they are purchased is another effort to avoid simony. This is to ensure that people will not think they are paying for the blessing. Though those who fashion a beautiful setting or reliquary from precious metals for the proper display of relics are justified in charging a price for the materials and the labor, there can be no question of paying for a relic, which is a holy object.

There are also more subtle examples of simony that persist to this day. We cannot, for instance, refuse the sacraments to people because they fail to support the Church financially or because they haven't leapt through some bureaucratic hoop, such as being regis-tered with the parish. God alone owns the spiritual goods, and He freely dispenses of them as He pleases, to and through the clergy and the people. Related to this are those who charge exorbitant fees for preaching or giving retreats. "You received without pay, give without pay" is an important admonition to keep in mind (Matt. 10:8).

In the past, ecclesiastical offices were often bought and sold: Bishoprics and abbeys and the like went to those who bid highest. Though it is dangerous to judge past practices by today's standards, selling benefices or ecclesiastical offices was and always is a sin. Even today there have been cases of men being made cardinals because they are excellent fund-raisers, even though they may lead scandalous lives. For a superior to look the other way in making ecclesiastical appointments and to take only secular utility into account would be simony.

Let's make one final distinction here: Mass stipends are not simony. When someone makes a donation for a Mass said for an intention, it is not a fee but a free-will expression of support for the minister and the church. Moreover, most dioceses set a suggested stipend for a Mass, and this must be interpreted as the diocese trying to protect the faithful by preventing parishes from asking exorbitant stipends. The clergy have a right to a livelihood from their spiritual works, but people should not be denied the spiritual good of offering a Mass if they cannot give a stipend.

All of these vices are against the nature of God, to Whom we owe reverence and fidelity. What is especially troubling about the vices of irreligion is that the person acknowledges the true God, but in his practices, he acts counter to this apparent knowledge. Since God demands in justice, let alone charity, the fullness of our respect and integrity, each of these vices corrupts the true order of peace with God that the soul was created to reflect.

The Third Commandment

Justice to God

We discussed at the beginning of this book how before the Fall, man's whole life involved a continuous worship of God. Indeed, some saints and theologians have argued that Adam, before the Fall, enjoyed a state of perpetually infused contemplation — a devout, reverent, adoring union with God. The Commandments, then, are about restoring this condition to which we are called in our humanity. The first two commandments address negative aspects of the virtue of religion — that is, expressions of irreligion that we are to avoid. The Third Commandment, however, shifts to positive expressions of the virtue of religion, by which we seek in our hearts and in our bodies to return to the authentic worship that Adam experienced at every moment.

We have said the virtue of religion is part of the virtue of justice. The clearest expression of this virtue is in interactions between equals, called "commutative justice" in Church documents. For instance: One signs a work contract with another person, and when the work is done, the contracting person must pay the contractor what was promised. For his part, the contractor guarantees an honest product. Buying a loaf of bread from a baker is an everyday example of commutative justice.

The Decalogue Decoded

But there are others to whom we owe rights whom we can never repay because there is no equality. Yet by natural law, in justice we are required to offer something as an attempt to compensate. The virtue of religion entails the attempts of man to repay God for all the gifts he has received. The interior and exterior acts by which we do this generally constitute true worship.

The first two commandments are progressively ordered to drawing the mind of man away from practices with respect to God that might compromise true worship. The Third Commandment addresses the positive practices of the virtue of religion that truly respect God and that must be reflected both in the soul and in action.

The aspects of religion required by this Third Commandment can be divided into *interior* and *exterior* expressions. The interior expressions of religion are *devotion* and *prayer*, and the exterior are *adoration* and *sacrifice*. Remember that while the Commandments talk principally about things we do with our bodies, they also address or presume the virtuous integrity of our souls supporting through charity — that is, love of God — our bodily actions. In the case of worshipping God, what we do with our bodies also supports the development of our souls.

The Third Commandment reads, "Remember the Sabbath day, to keep it holy" (Exod. 20:8), and it is not, as some have read it, only about some exterior formalism in practicing religion. Rather, in telling us to preserve the day of the Lord's rest, it commands us to express thanksgiving to God, which necessarily includes the interior acts of our souls. This commandment is both a moral commandment that has to do with the attitude of our hearts and a ceremonial commandment that has to do with the actions of our bodies. To become more fully human — to actualize most fully our nature as being made in God's image — we must set aside some time for the refreshment of our souls through the contemplation of divine things. This is because the spiritual soul must have actions that are exclusively reserved to it.

I once gave a retreat to Mother Teresa's sisters, the Sisters of Charity, and they told me it wasn't too hard to find people to help with their work for the poor. But when they asked volunteers to help them by spending a couple of hours in contemplation before the Blessed Sacrament, almost no one accepted. This Third Commandment, though, demands that, for some time during the week, we occupy our minds and our bodies in pursuing our interior union with God, which is the origin of the Sabbath rest.

Now, some Christian sects have debated when exactly the Sabbath should be celebrated. Jews celebrated the Sabbath on the seventh day — that is, Saturday — to commemorate God's resting in the work of creation and in anticipation of the fulfillment of that creation in the Messiah. In the New Law, we are still commanded to make time for contemplation and rest, but creation has been fulfilled in Jesus Christ, and so the day has been changed to the first day of the week, Sunday, commemorating the initial creation and the new creation in the Holy Spirit effected at Pentecost.

Purity and Peace

The Sabbath rest is to be marked by two conditions: purity and consecration to God. Purity refers to the unity of mind and heart that is preserved in one's body by resting in God. Maintaining the purity of our intentions demands, at the very least, that we withdraw once per week from the ordinary pursuits of human life, lest we become so caught up in worldly concerns that we never have that peaceful, integrated rest in God — and there we see the second condition, the consecration of the Sabbath to the Lord. This means that a person must abstain from certain activities on the Sabbath that would be lawful on other days.

The Decalogue Decoded

There are three aspects to securing this peace. First, we must avoid servile work, which is work that occupies the body as opposed to the mind. We should never be bound to do servile work on Sunday, aside from genuinely necessary work, such as preparing food for the family or public safety work or caring for the sick. Remember that Jesus cautioned against an overly strict, unrealistic reading of Sabbath prohibitions (see Matt. 12:1–14). Of course, if one's employer demands that one work on Sunday, even if the work is not strictly necessary, then the employee is bound to it—but the abuse of the Sabbath is the employer's, not the employee's.

It can be easy to become scrupulous about what servile work entails. The *Code of Canon Law* specifies that it is work "which interferes with the worship owed to God, the joy proper to the Lord's Day, the performance of the works of mercy and the appropriate relaxation of mind and body."[4] The *Catechism* refers to a distinction of Saint Augustine: "The charity of truth seeks holy leisure; the necessity of charity accepts just work."[5]

The Sabbath is, secondly, also to be a time especially free from interior desires that might conflict with peace in God. So, the avoidance of sin is also included in this precept. We are, of course, to seek to liberate ourselves from sinful desires all the time, but this day should be set aside for the purpose in a special way. To enslave oneself to material or other worldly desires is to make finding joy or rest in contemplation of God all but impossible. Connected with this idea, then, is the notion that the Sabbath, while a day of rest, is not a day of idleness. Often we find entire families, led by their fathers, parked in front of the television all Sunday to watch football games. This is not the leisure envisioned in the commandment but rather is trivial; the same goes for playing video games all day.

---

[4] See canon 120, quoted in CCC 2185.
[5] Saint Augustine, *De civitate Dei* 19, 19; quoted in CCC 2185.

Though this is not servile work, it is certainly not the Sabbath rest. Such activity distracts us from the contemplation we are called to, which requires direct, conscious attention to God.

This conscious attention then leads to the third aspect of Sabbath rest, which brings us full circle: that we keep the Lord's Day holy by performing works of consecration to God—both interior (devotion and prayer) and exterior (adoration and sacrifice). Beginning with the interior expressions, the word "devotion" comes from a Latin word *vovere*, which means "to vow." To take a vow means to give ourselves completely, willingly, and spontaneously to a task. This commandment, then, requires us to give ourselves totally to service of God and to have a will that is free to be directed by God as He sees fit. Attentiveness to the seemingly spontaneous movements of His will is of the very essence of the devout life and of internal acts of religion. One of the principal signs of this openness to spontaneity is the cheerfulness with which we give ourselves to God. Living a life of contemplation is not about being a sourpuss!

Saintly Spontaneity

A beautiful example of this openness and cheerfulness is Saint Lawrence, who was famously roasted alive by Roman authorities, during which he apparently quipped, "I'm done on this side. Please turn me over." But the events that preceded this demonstrate the saint's qualities even more winsomely. The Roman magistrate had demanded that Lawrence, in his capacity as deacon in the local church, bring to his palazzo "the treasure of the church." Lawrence agreed, and the next day, he presented to the magistrate the treasure: the poor, the blind, the lame, and the sick. It was for this that Lawrence was executed.

Loving devotion to God also requires having an awareness of our shortcomings. Meditating on these shortcomings brings us to a fuller appreciation of God's gifts, allowing us to respond to Him with that cheerful spontaneity that is so pleasing to Him and attractive to others. It can be hard to bring our shortcomings to prayer; it seems easier, and is quite common, to present to God a phony version of the self, a perfect image that we know (and He certainly knows) is not the real thing. We do not want to spontaneously express all our weaknesses, trials, and sorrows — but then we wonder why we make no progress in prayer! Being spontaneous and devout in the service of God demands that we bring ourselves as we really are before him.

Saint Teresa of Avila was once caught in a storm while traveling. When she got out of the coach, she fell in the mud, looked up to heaven, and said to God, "If this is the way You treat Your friends, no wonder You have so few!" This is spontaneous devotion! She turned to God immediately and, in a humorous way, presented her troubles to Him. In His time and in His way, we can and will stop worrying about our problems and will worry only about Him. To get there, though, we must joyfully offer all that we have and all that we are to Him.

This means, also, that devotion must be more than rote. Part of the justice entailed in the virtue of religion is forming our wills to give ourselves *readily* and *spontaneously* to divine service. One of the banes of all religious practice, including among those who have taken the vows of religion for the consecrated life, is to perform acts of religion with no openness or spontaneity because one lacks interior freedom.

Turning Directly to God

Once we have this devout and joyful union with God, we must express it in prayer, the second aspect of interior religious practice. This is an act of the intellect: Prayer in the intellect is the companion to devotion in the will, and together they form an integrated soul recognizing the majesty of God. We must feel free to ask for everything that we need from God. We must confess, as Saint Augustine did in his *Confessions*, that we rely upon God's aid for everything. This includes a constant prayer for actual grace. Even Adam needed the support of God before the Original Sin, and he needed to express the necessity of this support. The primary character of the Original Sin is that both Adam and Eve made a choice about the commandment they were given without praying to God to help them. Adam may have enjoyed perfect contemplation, but he also had to express continuously his devotion in his heart.

So, this commandment demands not only that we excite ourselves by devotion of heart but also that we give expression to this excitement and to the spontaneity of love in words addressed to God, expressing our dependence on Him for our every need. Those of us who pray the Liturgy of the Hours say, before most of the hours, a prayer that expresses this well: "O God, come to my assistance; Lord, make haste to help me!" And, of course, the most perfect prayer is that which Jesus taught us: the Lord's Prayer. These are not the only words we can say to fulfill the virtue of religion, but Christ tells us that in the seven petitions of the Our Father we find everything our prayer should express.

Bodily Reverence

The exterior acts of religion, you will remember, are adoration and sacrifice. Since man is not an angel, it is incumbent upon him that he express his interior devotion and prayer by external actions. This is one of the reasons why the Lord instituted sacraments, reflecting a famous Scholastic axiom: "The sacraments are for man." Catholicism is an intensely *incarnational* religion, affirming the fact that Christ's flesh is now a necessary tool by which we experience the presence and power of the Holy Spirit in our lives. On the Sabbath, then, man is called to adoration.

Adoration consists of bodily actions, including speech, by which we give due reverence to God and express to Him what is in our hearts. This kind of adoration, expressed by the Greek word *latria*, is due *only* to God, not to any creature. It is the kind of adoration we give to Jesus' human nature and, by extension, to the Blessed Sacrament. The genuflection demonstrates this in the Western Church, as does the profound bow in some Western rites and in the Eastern Church. As always, external signs of adoration are meant to encourage interior devotion and to express interior prayer. A professor of mine once said that people may describe their faith in the Blessed Sacrament with all the flowery words they want, but unless they're willing to genuflect reverently before the Host, they have not shown the fullness of their belief. The richness of the gestures we perform at Mass and in the presence of the Blessed Sacrament generally demonstrates our adoration for the Holy Trinity.

Some people accuse Catholics of worshipping the Virgin Mary, but we give her honor and reverence — expressed in the Greek as *hyperdulia* — not adoration. We venerate her, fulfilling the Scripture text: "All generations will call me blessed" (Luke 1:48). The saints, on the other hand, receive ordinary respect and veneration, which in Greek is called *dulia*.

On the Sabbath, we are called not only to adoration but even more to sacrifice. Sacrifice is also a necessary aspect of exterior religious practice. Indeed, three of the key ways we keep the Sabbath holy — sacrifice, almsgiving, and hearing the Word of God — are all present and summarized in the Holy Sacrifice of the Mass, which is Jesus' own act of prayer, devotion, and adoration. Though receiving Communion may be its culmination, the Mass is much more than a Communion service. It's an offering of ourselves in union with Christ's self-offering, the one Eternal Sacrifice that inspires and completes all prayer.

Mass: The Perfection of Religion — and the Sabbath

The essence of the Mass is both exterior and interior oblation. The exterior oblation is connected to the Eternal Sacrifice on the Cross in the distinct consecration of the bread and the wine. For in every sacrifice, one offers a gift back to God as a sign of the covenant that He has made with man and in recognition of our complete dependence on Him. In response, God accepts the victim, and the offering is sealed in His consecration and acceptance.

For this reason, assistance at Mass is made a law of the Church as the most perfect expression of keeping the Sabbath holy, since it makes the one Eternal Sacrifice of Christ present. At Mass, all the interior and exterior acts of prayer and worship are done by the Son of God, and we become a part of them! This Mass is an Eternal Act carried out in heaven that, through the ritual of the priest, becomes present to us. This ritual action is completed only in the Communion of the priest; if the priest receives Communion after the laity, the sacrifice is compromised.

Failure to attend Mass, therefore, is a failure to associate ourselves weekly with the very Sabbath rest that Christ now enjoys in God, with His Sacrifice accepted in heaven. This is a serious breach of Christian discipline. We must emphasize now and always that the fullness and completion of our duties in religion to God, expressed in the first tablet of the Commandments, is found in devotion, prayer, adoration, and sacrifice. It is not only about avoiding vices of irreligion, but also about taking positive actions toward union with Him. The sacrifice of the Mass is the place where this occurs *par excellence*.

This aspect of the Mass has perhaps been much eclipsed since Vatican II. Many want to reduce the Mass to a Communion service. The now-deceased Cardinal Alfons Maria Stickler, who attended Vatican II, had this to say:

> The essential center, the sacrificial action itself, suffered a perceptible shift toward Communion, in that the entire Sacrifice of the Mass was changed into a Eucharistic meal, whereby in the consciousness of believers the integrating component of Communion replaced the essential component of the transforming act of sacrifice.[6]

The Mass, in fact, makes present the Sacrifice of the Cross, offered by Christ the High Priest, which is eternal in its effect. Christ is said to be "a high priest for ever after the order of Melchizedek," who was "without father or mother or genealogy, and has neither beginning of days nor end of life" (Heb. 6:20; 7:3). Christ as man does not need to be ordained a priest. He is *Messiah* and *Christ* by His very nature because of the Hypostatic Union, so His humanity itself is holy. He can never lose this unique grace.

Christ is the eternal High Priest and "King of Righteousness" because He is full of grace and brings righteousness to us. He is "King of Peace" because He not only brings the peace of order back to our souls through grace, but also because He brings peace to the human race through the society of the Church, His Body.

The Sacrifice of Christ is unique because He is both Priest and Victim. His sacrifice is more than just a repetition of the Last Supper; it includes the Passion and Resurrection. The Mass does not make up for anything lacking in the Cross; instead, during the time it is celebrated, we participate in our space and time in the

[6] Alfons Cardinal Stickler, "Recollections of a Vatican II Peritus," *Latin Mass Magazine* (Winter 1999).

once-and-for-all Sacrifice of Calvary. As the Council of Trent says: "The priest is the same, the victim is the same, only the manner of offering is different" (Session 22). The Cross is the bloody offering; the Mass is the unbloody offering.

The primary priest at every Mass is Christ, and the human priest is merely His visible minister. And each Mass is not a successive sacrifice; rather, it makes Calvary present to us as part of a single, uninterrupted action of offering. The purpose of this Sacrifice is the same as that of all sacrifices: the glorification of God. Christ, who continually intercedes with the Father for us from heaven, is made present. So, each Mass is truly heaven on earth.

There are two aspects of the gift of self—the oblation—in the offering of the Mass. There is first the exterior sacrifice that we can see and touch, which is made present by transubstantiation in the consecration of the elements of bread and wine. Then there is the interior oblation. To the extent that we spiritually identify with the obedience and love of Christ, Who becomes present through the action of the ministerial priest, we offer ourselves with Him. This is divine worship. Christ's obedience and love transform us and become our own. We grow in grace, obedience, and charity.

This is the active participation so dear to the fathers at Vatican II. It does not mean constant noise, singing, and carrying on so that the believer cannot have a quiet thought. Active participation means a most holy moment in which one mystically encounters the God-Man in contemplation. Where only action is emphasized, the human element obscures the divine, and man, who thirsts for God, comes away spiritually unsatisfied. Though singing and dialogue can aid in this, they cannot substitute for the inner silence of the heart.

So, the Third Commandment demands that we assist at Mass on Sunday and holy days. Though Communion is the fullness of participation in the sacrament, it is not commanded. There is a value to spiritual attendance at the Sacrifice even if one does not receive physical Communion.

Now, the Mass glorifies God not only as an act of praise and thanksgiving but also by expiation and appeal. The Church's application of the infinite love of Christ's Sacrifice can be helpful to the living who repent and the dead who have died repentant and are in purgatory. The sacrifice of appeal and expiation consists of conferring supernatural gifts on others, and is, in a sense, finite because it is applied to human beings. The sacrifice of praise and adoration, on the other hand, is infinite because God is infinite. This is the reason one can offer multiple Masses for the same intention, as when one offers several Masses for the repose of someone's soul.

Christ's treasury of merit and love are applied in a special way to those for whom the Mass stipend is given, and the priest has an important responsibility in justice to be sure that all Masses for which stipends have been given are said. This treasury of merit extends from the saints to the living and the dead. The offering and Communion at Mass have one purpose: the glorification of God, as the Church offers herself constantly with Christ.

This Sacrifice is the culmination of the virtue of religion required by the first three commandments. In the Mass, we find the perfect expression of the attempt to give all things back to God for His glory. "What shall I render to the LORD for all his bounty to me? I will lift up the cup of salvation and call on the name of the LORD" (Ps. 116:12–13).

The Fourth Commandment

The Second Tablet

Now we move on to the second tablet of the Ten Commandments, from those that refer to God to those that refer to our neighbor. While our relationship with our Creator is the foundation of being elevated back to union with Him, that relationship must be reflected in our dealings with our fellow human beings. That begins with those who are closest to us.

The virtue of religion, by which we do justice by trying to repay God in some incomplete but real way for His gifts, has companion virtues. Related to our devotion to God is treating with dignity those who are His images. "Let us not love in word or speech but in deed and in truth" (1 John 3:18). We must therefore avoid acts that are evil with respect not only to God but also to our neighbor—and do acts that are good not only for God but also for our neighbor. Some have observed that none of the Ten Commandments tell us to love our neighbor, but the Fourth Commandment more or less says just this.

The Virtue of Piety

Loving our neighbor begins with loving those closest to us—specifically those who brought us into the world, who worked and

47

sacrificed and sometimes suffered for us. These are the people specifically mentioned in the Fourth Commandment: "Honor your father and your mother" (Exod. 20:12). The virtue by which we give honor and respect and reverence to those who have done the most for us is piety. This virtue is related to religion in that it is about justly repaying the gifts given to us, but rather than being directed toward God, it is directed toward other persons and communities who act in His place in our lives: parents, other relatives, superiors in the Church, our country, and even sometimes our friends. This is expressed in positive terms in this commandment whereas the next four proscribe vices against the love of neighbor.

Piety, in this context, simply means a loving, generous giving of ourselves to those who have given themselves to us in ways we can never adequately repay. It is a virtue that seems to be in short supply today. But just think about the way human relationships work, and you'll see how essential it is. Our parents are co-creators of us with God; we received the gift of life from them. To ignore that would be tremendously ungrateful! It is true that it might be impossible to repay this incredible gift fully, but that is why we show our parents honor and, up to a certain age, obedience: This is simple justice. If honor and respect are not shown to those who have given us the gift of life, everything falls apart.

Further, since this commandment is a response in gratitude to favors received, it includes an obligation to perform deeds of kindness and mercy. These are not explicitly enumerated, but they are included by extension from the kindness one owes oneself. Remember the second great commandment according to Our Lord: "Love your neighbor as you love yourself" (Lev. 19:18). The consideration we give ourselves, and with which we would like to be treated, we must extend to all, especially to those to whom we owe much.

Now, extensions of our parents would be, for instance, the society in which we live, the community that has supported us.

This can mean the nation, but it also means smaller (and bigger) societies that have provided the ability for us to carry on our lives in peace and order. This is the common good, or the commonweal, and seeking that together with fellow members of society means honoring the authority, the civil society, the *patria* (or "fatherland") that binds us together.

Finally, we owe piety to anyone who has given us those deeply human gifts that we are unable to repay in their fullness—affection, friendship, loving service. These friends share in maintaining our happiness and quality of life in ways that are impossible to calculate. But to appreciate this, we have to love ourselves—not in the sense of a disordered narcissism, but in the respect, the appreciation, even the awe that we must have for the goodness of *our own* being. We cannot appreciate what others have done for us without appreciating what God has done for us in creating us: We have to love our own dignity before we can honor others for respecting and fostering it.

Being Is Good

We have to understand that it is good that we exist! This might seem obvious, but in today's day and age, with so much despair and nihilism, it really isn't. The loss of appreciation for the self, which comes from losing sight of the fact that we come from the hands of a loving Creator, is in part responsible for the breakdown of the family, which, in turn, leads to the breakdown of authority generally. We first experience the goodness of our existence by affection and truthful affirmation from our parents, but this truth can be distorted or suppressed by parents who do not know how to be parents.

Many times, when I taught high school, I watched fathers become extremely angry at their sons for their performance at some task or game, teaching the lesson that the goodness of these boys was contingent on their success. I remember going to ball games and hearing fathers yelling obscenities at their sons because they had a bad performance. I could see the clenched teeth of these children—they were still boys, after all—reacting to their fathers, who were, in a sense, condemning their existence, making them feel as if they were worthless if they did not succeed.

It has been lamented that the Ten Commandments don't include a reference to kindness and gentleness, but right here in the Fourth, we find the source of kindness and gentleness—as an extension of the authentic love and appreciation one should have toward oneself.

Corruptions of Family Life

Let us look more closely at the relationship of parents to children. First, while a mother and a father are necessary to create a child, they are not enough. The soul is a spiritual principle, and it requires the direct work of God to bring it into existence. The work of the parents together with God is traditionally called "procreation" because parents are permitted to participate with God in a new creation. The attempt to reduce this relationship to simply reproduction makes the process mechanistic and materialistic, and the child nothing more than the product of the will of his or her parents. This is the way of thinking about childbearing that leads directly to the mainstreaming of artificial contraception and assisted reproductive technologies. As *Gaudium et Spes* states: "Man is the only being willed for his own sake."[7]

---

[7] Second Vatican Council, Pastoral Constitution on the Church in the Modern World *Gaudium et Spes* (December 7, 1965), no. 24.

The contraceptive mentality leads to the assumption that the value of a person, whether a spouse or a child, is that person's usefulness to another. We no longer think, "You are good because you exist," but, "You are good because you make me feel good." Thus, the parents become objects manipulated by each other's wills, and the child becomes an object manipulated by his parents. Everybody tries to use one another. The child then receives the impression that he is loved not simply because he exists but because of what he accomplishes. This reduces the child's self-respect to something he must assert for himself, a kind of will to power, and thus he resists discipline. Lacking that natural self-respect and natural love for his existence, the child struggles to receive discipline as a gift from his parents, by which they try to turn him away from the bad and toward the good. Instead, discipline becomes a power contest between the child and his parents. This begins in the family and is carried into the schools and into the streets.

So many of our social problems come from manipulation and lack of love in the family. Discipline must flow, *both* from parents to children *and* from children to parents, as part of a relationship in which each recognizes the image of God in the other and in himself. Since parents are the source of both the existence and the nurturing of their children, they reflect the objective and unchanging love of a powerful yet merciful God and thus enable their children to learn naturally to love themselves and others in the same way.

And so, properly understood, parents represent God to their children because they participated in giving them life, and because they provide for and sacrifice for them. It makes sense that we should honor those who reflect God's love for us in a special way. The same is true of our country. The civil authority, again, properly understood, exercises its authority in the name of God. This doesn't mean that every law has to be sealed in the name of the Trinity (though that would be nice); it does mean that all legitimate authority ultimately comes from God. He is the Source of the civil authority, and so a proper relationship with Him requires respect—that is, piety—for earthly authority.

The Duties, Rights, and Limits of Authority

The civil authorities are owed and receive this respect not as individual persons, but by reason of their office, by which they represent the common good. By the peace and order that civil authorities provide, God establishes justice through the natural order in everyday human relationships. Not every action or power of man falls under this authority, though—only those that are connected to the social common good, which is not the sum total of the individual goods of citizens but a deeper good than individuals can attain on their own. The foundation of the common good is the dignity of each person, and thus the right to life.

So, this is important: No earthly authority, whether the state or one's parents, can justly command a citizen to violate God's law, to harm the order of love, to sin, and so forth. We can't say, "My country is wrong" or "My parents are wrong." These authorities must themselves respect the authority God has placed in the world, and from which they derive their force. The virtues of piety and religion do not conflict; to disregard a command from the lower authority that contradicts God is not a violation of piety, but a higher form of it.

This also has important implications for the origin of authority. The civil authority is uniquely deputized to speak for and to implement the common good, and all communities need authority to direct and to encourage members to pursue the shared good of all. Therefore, no authority exists to perpetuate or to affirm only itself: It is always at the service of the community.

Sins committed by people in authority have a greater weight because they create scandal and lead the community astray. As a result, those who exercise authority are held to a higher standard than other members of the community. A good community must ensure checks and balances on the manner in which authority is exercised. Otherwise, the members of the community will have no ability to defend their rights or to seek justice if their rights are violated. Since obedience is primarily a matter of intellect and is implemented only in the will, truth, which is apprehended in the intellect, cannot be determined simply at the arbitrary whim or oppressive will of the authority. Men are thus reduced to a herd; communities must be ready to counteract this impulse.

Sometimes in communities in which authority comes from nature, such as the family, an abuse of authority can be remedied only by the interference of a higher community. In this case, the state has a right and duty to interfere for the good of the victims of the oppressive authority. But it must be emphasized that this is exceptional and should be done only in extreme circumstances. Finally, the morality of resistance to civil authority is very difficult to determine; it must be exercised with great discretion. Though one must love and honor one's country, there are limits, in justice, to what one must bear. The unbridled nationalism of the nineteenth and early twentieth centuries, for instance, does not correspond to the virtue of piety.

God Trumps

In the home and in society, then, religion trumps piety. Here's an example: Sometimes parents oppose the entrance of their children into the religious life or the priesthood. Saint Catherine of Siena's mother wanted her to marry a rich man, and she pestered her daughter so much that Catherine cut off her hair to make herself unattractive to men. Thomas Aquinas's family imprisoned him in a tower for two years because they did not want him to become a Dominican. (It would have been all right with them if he wanted to join a wealthy order, but not the mendicant Order of Preachers.) And you'll remember that Jesus told His Apostles that family members would become enemies due to Him (see Matt. 10:35; 19:29).

The duty to honor God in the virtue of religion comes prior to the duty of piety, and so familial concerns should not stop someone who has reached the age of twenty-one from pursuing a religious vocation. Now, if one's parents need financial or medical or other personal support that a child must provide, then this would probably be a sign that one doesn't have a vocation to enter religious life. But parents' mere resistance to the idea is not necessarily binding on their child.

Parental Duties

The family is also the domestic church, so the rights and duties of piety touch directly on charity. After all, Jesus chose to be born into an ordinary human family characterized by affection and love; He is present in a special way in family life.

The duties of parents include, in a special way, education in the virtues. "The right and duty of parents to educate their children are primordial and inalienable" (CCC 2221).[8] For parents, this must include realizing that they are instruments of God's love, and so they must first be obedient to Him in managing the family and in their manner of exercising discipline. They are to teach "self-denial, sound judgment, and self-mastery," and if they cannot exercise these virtues themselves, it is near impossible to impart them to their children (CCC 2223).

---

[8] Cf. John Paul II, Apostolic Exhortation *Familiaris Consortio* (November 22, 1981), no. 36.

Parents are also the first apostles for their children. The teaching and manner of living religion in the home is the foundation for the child's idea of God. This should include a loving and affectionate mother in the primary years and a strong and truthful but merciful father in the adolescent years. These obligations are guaranteed by the fact that the state, in justice, cannot force the parents into an education system against their morals.

This right to choose should also extend to the option to home-school. Some dioceses have attempted to create guidelines for homeschoolers, even requiring they become licensed catechists to prepare their children to receive the sacraments. Though pastors and bishops certainly have a right and a duty to demand that children be well prepared for the reception of the sacraments, parents need no license from anyone to do this: They are licensed by God as pro-creators with Him!

Discipline is a key to the formation of a mature person; after all, God disciplines us. Let's consider two brief selections from Scripture: "Whoever loves a son will chastise him often.... Whoever disciplines a son will benefit from him" (Sir. 30:1, 2, NABRE). "Fathers, do not provoke your children to anger, but bring them up in the discipline and instruction of the Lord" (Eph. 6:4). Catholics have never been of the school of thought that children must have the depravity of the devil beaten out of them. Rather, following Christ and Greek philosophy, Catholics have respected the child as a person who may be weak but is always generally ordered to the good. Exaggerated punishments have never been Catholic.

The Fruits of Piety

Life cannot be reduced to strict justice. There are two aspects of living out the virtue of piety that make life better. These are not strictly demanded in justice, but they are part of living a more fully human life and building lasting and genuinely good communities. These are *observance*, by which we honor persons in positions of excellence in the community, and *gratitude*, by which we seek to return thanks to our benefactors.

Observance demands that we respect — both exteriorly and interiorly, as with God — our human superiors, whether civil or ecclesial. Now, as we said, human superiors are to be obeyed and honored only up to the limits of their authority; they cannot justly command sin. Honoring them fittingly recognizes that administering a community is a burden of office for which one can never be fully repaid. Even though a superior may be unscrupulous, we still owe this honor, even if we might feel differently about it than we would if the leader were more virtuous. When I honor my superior in my order or the president, I am not honoring him as an individual; rather, I'm honoring the community through his office. The observance and respect we give to these superiors acknowledge that we're all dependent on each other in this struggle of life.

In the eighteenth and nineteenth centuries, the "social contract" theory of political authority burst onto the scene. According to this theory, authority could be justly exercised only with the agreement of the people. Instead of reflecting God's authority, leaders were said to be reflecting *the people's* authority. *The people* determined what was right or wrong, just or unjust. Thus, the people had no natural dependence on anyone, and they could take away authority from their leaders if they wanted to. This is not what the Ten Commandments teach us. Though we have a right to determine who precisely will exercise authority in our society, that authority is rooted in the truth and goodness of God, not in our will.

Getting this wrong has led to a great deal of trouble. It seems that there's a complete void of respect for authority in the Western world today, and the will to power seems to be the only organizing principle in our social relationships. Instead of mutual service, we are interested only in mutual use, mutual exploitation. This impacts both the authority and those who are the subjects of authority. Bossing and being bossed are not expressions of genuine leadership; they're expressions of contempt.

The sin against this aspect of the commandment, against the proper commands of a superior, is that of disobedience. This is a serious sin because it involves not only disregard for the law, but also contempt for the ability of the superior to make such a law. Now, disobedience is not as grave as murder or blasphemy because it involves only contempt for the lawgiver; these other sins involve contempt for the nature of the law as well.

The Limits of Calculation

As for gratitude, the world cannot be directed only on a tit-for-tat basis, on giving only as much as we have received. There must be some initial effort, some going above and beyond the mere dictates of equity, in the materialist sense. The world must be governed by positive efforts of mutual respect and honor, the recognition that even our lives are gifts received from others. God showers us continuously with blessings—and so do others. I heard of a woman who wrote on a calendar the special favors she received from a friend each day. At the end of the month, she looked at the calendar and thanked God for each of those persons and wrote them letters to thank them. The psychological value of this exercise should be evident: When we give thanks to another, we appreciate how loved we are, and we want to give as we have received.

Many things that are necessary for the maintenance of a good human life and strong communities—friendliness, liberality, affability, and even kindness—are not commanded in strict justice. It is not usually just or even possible to punish violations of these by the civil law, but they are necessary for the upkeep of any society.

The Decalogue Decoded

The value of having people around you who are kind to one another is impossible to tabulate, as we all recognize that in the struggle of this earthly life, we are all in it together, all striving to maintain that interior union and integrity that brings us closer to God. Just as one cannot live in society without truth, so one cannot live in society without joy.

Likeability may seem a strange virtue, but Teresa of Avila recommended it to her nuns. She said that if we want others to imitate our virtues, we need to be accessible:

> This is very important for nuns: the holier they are, the more sociable they should be with their sisters.... Never keep aloof from them if you wish to help them and have their love. We must strive hard to be pleasant and to humor the people we deal with and make them like us, especially our sisters.[9]

Finally, the virtue of gratitude — of simply saying thanks to one another, of maintaining a gracious disposition, of realizing that little acts of service are genuine gifts to us — brings out all these other habits of sociability that make community possible. The world cannot be run by the spirit of pure calculation of the world's bureaucracy and administration. It demands that we give honor and gratitude — that is, piety — to all those who have given to us.

[9] Saint Teresa of Avila, *The Way of Perfection*, chap. 41.

The Fifth Commandment

The Grace of the "Negative" Commandments

Beginning here, with the Fifth, the Commandments of the second tablet are expressed in a negative way — as strict prohibitions rather than positive commands. Of course, though, they must be read in the context of the first four: They react, in a sense, to the positive commandments concerning God and our neighbor. These negative commandments generally forbid injury done to other persons, who are made in the image of God.

Let's begin, though, by addressing two modern arguments that undercut these "negative" commandments. The first is the idea that no commandment can be truly universal because the Spirit may inspire us to set aside the "letter of the law" in specific situations. Now, this does come from a genuine principle in Catholic teaching called *epikeia*, but this is not about setting aside the law; rather, it is about reading a situation to see how the law should be applied. So, though there are often situations (as we will discuss) in which the application of the law is not obvious, this is a question of our limited understanding, not of the limits of the law. The letter of the law is always ordered to the Spirit; it cannot be "overruled" by that same Spirit. If we were meant merely to discern the will of the Spirit in every situation, the Law itself would be superfluous.

Though it is true that the civil law may be imperfect in the manner in which it is promulgated and applied, this can never be true of the natural law. The natural law is the application of reason to the question of the actions that befit human nature, as it has been made by the mind of the Creator. All of the commandments except the Ninth and the Tenth are connected as such to justice.

Secondly, some will point to moments in Scripture when God apparently violates or contradicts His own commandments. The Jews were commanded to despoil the Egyptians; Abraham was commanded to sacrifice his son; Hosea was commanded to marry a harlot. But these do not mean that His commandments are not absolute: After all, God is the very author and order of nature! He, and He alone, can dispense from His Law; because He has done so does not mean that everything is up in the air for us. Further, His ability to overrule the Law is itself limited by the principle of noncontradiction. Thus, it is traditionally said that God can dispense from the second tablet of the Law — that is, the Commandments about our relationship with creatures — but not the first tablet, since those Commandments implicate His very nature.

One further point is important: Positive commandments, such as the Third and Fourth, do not have to be applied always and in every circumstance. One does not have to love one's parents in every act because one's parents are not always around. Negative commandments, such as the Fifth through the Eighth, on the other hand, are always active and binding.

The Dignity of (Human) Life

Now, let us examine the sin condemned in the Fifth Commandment: "You shall not kill" (Exod. 20:13). Every human person, because he has an immortal soul willed into existence by God, has the right to life. There is something ineffably dignified about the human person. Man is a spirit, and so he transcends matter; this transcendence must be respected and recognized in our actions. The most serious violation, then, that can be committed against a human person is to attack his very life. Murder strikes, quite literally, at the very heart of our dignity. This right to life is not and cannot be based on some calculation of other values; there are no other goods we can add together to amount to the good of one human life. There is no good that we can rightly pursue that is worth destroying an innocent life.

The *Catechism* addresses the sin of murder in these terms: "No one can under any circumstance claim for himself the right directly to destroy an innocent human being" (2258). The *Catechism* further specifies this using text from Scripture: "Do not slay the innocent and the righteous" (Exod. 23:7). Therefore: "The deliberate murder of an innocent person is gravely contrary to the dignity of the human being, to the golden rule, and to the holiness of the Creator. The law forbidding it is universally valid: it obliges each and every one, always and everywhere" (2261).

There are a few important considerations that will help us to better understand this seemingly straightforward commandment. The first is that it does not apply to animals, who have no reasoning soul. Everything in the lower orders of creation exists for the higher order: animals for humans, plants for animals and humans, and so on. Now, killing an animal may still be a sin, such as if the animal is the property of another, in which case it is a kind of theft; or if one is intentionally cruel to an animal, which disregards the goodness of creation and is often the acting out of a cruel disposition toward humans. But we cannot speak of a "right to life" for animals; their primary earthly purpose is to sustain our lives. One can be cruel to an animal, but not unjust.

The Decalogue Decoded

Guilt and Innocence

Now, there are a few other misinterpretations of this commandment that are difficult and need to be made clear: killing by the
state, killing the self, and killing in self-defense. The Fifth Commandment establishes the right to *innocent life*, so obeying it would
include the *defense* of innocent life. This would mean that a state
killing through capital punishment or just warfare or the just application of force by a police officer would be not violating but
affirming the right to life guaranteed by this commandment. This
would also be true of self-defense if the only way to preserve one's
life is by the death of the aggressor.

Suppose a person seeks private revenge, in society or at war,
through killing. This would be entirely different, since it would not
be the state acting in its capacity as the legitimate civil authority.
This would be a person, even if he were an officer of the state, such
as a police officer, acting on the motive of private revenge, and he
would be guilty of murder. This would include vigilante violence.

The death penalty has become a much-disputed question, even
by the Holy See. Catholic tradition has always stated that the
punishment must fit the crime and so conferred on the state the
right and, at times, the duty to invoke the death penalty for capital
murder. In the interest of preserving the life of innocents, an officer
of the state or, in war, a soldier may lawfully invoke the penalty
of death. Indeed, the repentant capital murderer should *want* to
undergo the death penalty, as an affirmation of his own right to
innocent life, which he has alienated by his crime. Only in this
way could the order of justice be satisfied.

Now, politically, I'm not recommending a vote for or against the
death penalty. Some today question its wisdom because of serious
injustices and the harrowing experience of totalitarian regimes in
the twentieth century. But their objection must be grounded not
on justice, rightly understood, or on the Fifth Commandment, but

on psychology. It simply can't be reasonably sustained that aborting an innocent baby and killing a guilty felon are the same kind of act, any more than it would be to say that cutting off a healthy limb is the same as cutting off a gangrenous one.

Recently, however, a number of Church authorities have maintained that capital punishment has been demonstrated to be as evil as abortion. In fact, the claim goes, if one is going to be against abortion, one must also be against capital punishment because both involve the death of a human person. This is called the "seamless garment" theory, invoking the robe of Christ, which was not torn by the Romans who played dice for it at the foot of the Cross. Let's consider where this view stands in the contemporary Church.

The *Catechism of the Catholic Church*, reflecting Pope John Paul II's teaching in *Evangelium Vitae*, summarized Church teaching on the death penalty by maintaining:

> Assuming that the guilty party's identity and responsibility have been fully determined, the traditional teaching of the Church does not exclude recourse to the death penalty, if this is the only possible way of effectively defending human lives against the unjust aggressor. (2267)

It went on to clarify:

> Today, in fact, as a consequence of the possibilities which the state has for effectively preventing crime, by rendering one who has committed an offense incapable of doing harm — without definitively taking away from him the possibility of redeeming himself — the cases in which the execution of the offender is an absolute necessity "are very rare, if not practically nonexistent."[10] (2267)

---

[10] John Paul II, *Evangelium Vitae* (March 25, 1995), no. 56.

The Decalogue Decoded

This would seem, at first glance, to be a clear case in which the teaching of the Church has changed according to the culture. If one looks closely though, one can see that the traditional teaching is affirmed that capital punishment accords with the natural law and is, in fact, in accord with human nature if properly applied. The issue raised by John Paul II is that of the circumstances in modern prison systems, which may make death an unnecessary and unreasonable means for affirming the right of innocent life. These circumstances can change and can be an object of debate. The fundamental moral teaching is still based on the authority of reason and faith experiencing and considering an unchanging human nature. If the death penalty need not be applied any longer, this is not because the culture has given us a new insight into human nature that the Church had never understood; it is rather because the circumstances of prison systems have made this penalty unnecessary for what its objective purpose has always been.

Pope Francis, however, has gone even further than Pope John Paul II. His position has led to a change in the text of the *Catechism* quoted above, which now reads, quoting the Holy Father:

> Recourse to the death penalty on the part of legitimate authority, following a fair trial, was long considered an appropriate response to the gravity of certain crimes and an acceptable, albeit extreme, means of safeguarding the common good.
>
> Today, however, there is an increasing awareness that the dignity of the person is not lost even after the commission of very serious crimes. In addition, a new understanding has emerged of the significance of penal sanctions imposed by the state. Lastly, more effective systems of detention have been developed, which ensure the due protection of citizens but, at the same time, do not definitively deprive the guilty of the possibility of redemption.

Consequently, the Church teaches, in the light of the Gospel, that "the death penalty is inadmissible because it is an attack on the inviolability and dignity of the person" and she works with determination for its abolition worldwide.[11]

A letter to the bishops affirmed that this is a genuine development of doctrine. One can see here the desire to affirm the inviolability of the dignity of the human person. But even with this development, we should consider the words of then-Cardinal Josef Ratzinger drawing a sharp distinction between capital punishment and objective crimes such as abortion:

> Not all moral issues have the same moral weight as abortion and euthanasia. For example, if a Catholic were at odds with the Holy Father on the application of capital punishment or on a decision to wage war, he would not for that reason be considered unworthy to present himself to receive Holy Communion. While the Church exhorts civil authorities to seek peace, not war, and to exercise discretion and mercy in imposing punishment on criminals, it may still be permissible to take up arms to repel an aggressor or to have recourse to capital punishment. There may be a legitimate diversity of opinion even among Catholics about waging war and applying the death penalty, but not however with regard to abortion and euthanasia.[12]

Further, the *Catechism* did not change the definition of murder from the direct killing of an innocent person. The only conclusion,

[11] "New Revision of Number 2267 of the *Catechism of the Catholic Church* on the Death Penalty," Vatican Press Office (August 2, 2018).

[12] Josef Cardinal Ratzinger, Letter to Theodore Cardinal McCarrick and Bishop Wilton Gregory (June 2004), reprinted in *L'Espresso* (July 2004).

therefore, is that this development of doctrine will demand greater care to address the need to protect society and to affirm the dignity of every life. As it stands, there can still be disagreement about the relative evil of killing innocent versus guilty persons with the sanction of the state, and about what the circumstances in a given state require of criminal justice.

No Right to Die

We should also note that suicide is forbidden by the Fifth Commandment. We are to love the image of God in ourselves. To seek to end one's life because one's material quality of life has been compromised or because of physical suffering completely ignores the proper order of the human soul: The body was made for the soul, and the soul was made for God. We see in Job, for example, a man who has lost all physical dignity, but who has not lost God or the dignity of his soul, and therefore what it means to be human. Euthanasia and physician-assisted suicide, of course, are also violations of this commandment because they mistake what the order and meaning of human life really are. When we think we can take our own lives, it implies that we are the lords over life and death, and God is not.

Though the Church wisely recognizes today that there may be emotional states that lead to a reduction of responsibility for suicides and thus no longer refuses them burial in consecrated ground, the objective truth remains that suicide leads to the death of an innocent person. It also deprives society of needed examples of suffering. In the case of suicides among young people, very prevalent in America today, it is necessary for proper family life both to protect the persons who think death is the only way to end their emotional pain and to ensure the proper development of society by not depriving the common good of those who might advance it.

The Fifth Commandment

Double Effect

Personal acts of self-defense are a tricky application of this commandment. We must understand that the Law forbids the killing of *innocent* persons. An assailant has voided that innocence. Defense must be proportionate to the threat, however: To intentionally kill a man armed with nothing but his fists is still murder. Intention, as we just said, is also important. The Church holds a principle called "double effect," in which an action has two foreseeable consequences, but the actor fully intends only one of those effects. In the case of self-defense, one might use deadly force to stop a deadly threat with the *intention* only to end the threat but the *knowledge* that his action might result in death. This is the proper interior posture toward self-defense; to actively *intend* the death of the assailant, on the other hand, would be permissible only if killing were the only way to stop the threat to the innocent life of the person or of someone else.

While the Fifth Commandment directly addresses only intentional killing, by implication it also condemns states of mind that might result in deadly violence. Consider, for instance, driving under the influence of drugs or alcohol. The person who drives drunk might not directly intend to kill, but he sins against this commandment through his reckless disregard for others' lives. This commandment, therefore, forbids putting oneself in a state in which he would be so irrational that he might not consider another's dignity and right to life.

Understanding Anger

This brings us to anger, which is a very urgent problem today. Anger can lead to a state of soul in which we become callous to the rights and dignity of others—even to the point of desiring or seeking their deaths. Now, anger is not evil in itself. There is lawful, ordered anger and unjust, disordered anger. Indeed, sometimes justice demands anger—that is, righteous anger at violence or exploitation—though not often does it require the exterior expression of that anger. Rather, we are to channel that passion in an orderly way into actions that seek to redress the injustice and promote the common good.

Those who express their anger in a disordered way often trample on the rights of others, failing to address the original injustice—as the wrongdoer hears not reason but only emotion—and often creating another injustice. Many people do this just to get rid of the feeling of anger. The commandment therefore also forbids encouraging ourselves to be so wrapped up in seeking affirmation of our own good that our emotions cloud our judgment as to what is good for another. If it is to be ordered and just, anger must be about correcting the other. The beginning of unjust killing is disordered anger, and the beginning of this anger is very often a disordered self-love.

Anger can overthrow reason, leading us to act irrationally. Remember Edgar Allan Poe's gothic story "The Cask of Amontillado," in which the main character responds to an insult by taking the man to his cellar, getting him drunk, and slowly bricking him up in a wall. All the while, the angry tormentor savors every moment as he listens to his insulter suffocate. This is an extreme example, but we can all remember times when our anger has driven us to desire that pain or another harm come to another person. This kind of anger can thus be either a mortal or a venial sin, depending on how much we cultivate it and what kind of act it leads us to perform.

What are some ways we can cure our anger—not to get rid of it, but to place it under the control of reason? First, we can work on not becoming angry easily or quickly. This kind of immediate response is almost never controlled by reason. It's cliché, but simply counting to ten can be of great help here. In the moment, we don't want to delay even for that little bit—but that should be a sign that reason is not in control. Second, we should work not to remain angry for long. Once the injustice has been resolved, let it go. Anger can fester and metastasize into worse passions, such as hatred. We must avoid hatred of others at all costs. Third, it is rarely a good idea to express our internal anger with words of anger to others, which cannot be fully taken back. We must always distinguish between the feeling and the expression of anger. Lastly, anger can provoke us to avoid undertaking deeds of mercy and justice. Choosing to act well toward others, even and especially those we are angry with, can help to order that anger well, under the dominion of reason.

Some credible Catholic psychiatrists have recognized that anger is a normal and natural emotion, but also that its expression needs to be humanely formed. The purpose of anger is the defense of the good against evil, and so there are indeed proper ways to go about expressing anger. But the Lord knew that even when these are well developed, we would all find occasions in which, for whatever reason, we could not obtain proper recompense for the evil done to us by another. We are then left with two choices: Either hold on to the anger and let it curdle and destroy us or make a conscious choice to forgive the evildoer and to let it go. The proper Christian response is the latter. This is perhaps why our good Physician Jesus placed the requirement in the Lord's Prayer that we are forgiven only to the extent that we forgive others.

Indeed, often in Christian history the forgiveness of a wrongdoer has led to his conversion. As Saint Stephen was being stoned, in imitation of Christ he prayed that God would forgive those who stoned him—among whom was Saul of Tarsus, later the remarkable Saint Paul. Paul's conversion has always been attributed by Christians to Stephen's prayers. And in the contemporary world, there is Saint Maria Goretti. While being stabbed for refusing sex to a housemate from another family, she told him: "Alessandro, do not do this. It is a sin and I want you to be with me in heaven forever." As she lay dying, she prayed that he would convert and be with her in heaven — and Alessandro eventually did repent and convert, dying in a Capuchin monastery. When questioned by a journalist if he despaired of his salvation because of the murder, he simply said that, but for the prayers and forgiveness of Maria Goretti, he would.

The Divine Physician

The Fifth Commandment, then, forbids not only the act of taking the life of an innocent human person, but also putting ourselves in a state in which it would be easy to forget or to ignore the rights and dignity of others. The best physician to heal our passions is the One Who became angry but never sinned. Like any good doctor, He teaches us to catch it early.

The Sixth Commandment

One Flesh

In the last chapter, we discussed the Fifth Commandment as an attack on the substance of the human person. Turning now to the Sixth Commandment, we discuss an attack on two persons who have so joined themselves together to become one: "You shall not commit adultery" (Exod. 20:14). The sin of adultery and all the other sins against the Sixth Commandment attack the most intimate sharing of human love and life experienced on earth. Marriage was instituted by God as the closest and deepest of natural human friendships.

In the natural order (we will speak later about the sacramental order) God instituted marriage in the book of Genesis. Even marriage vowed before a civil magistrate is a participation in the marriage that was founded by God at the beginning. Many Protestant denominations recognize such marriage as Christian, and since the ministers of marriage are the couple, not the clergy, these marriages are sacramental for the spouses so long as they are baptized. Catholics, of course, because of our idea of the Church, are bound to the Catholic form: Purely civil marriages, if not witnessed by an ordained minister of the Catholic Church, would not participate in marriage as founded by God.

The Decalogue Decoded

God's Plan for Marriage

God had given Adam the responsibility for participating in the destiny of his own life; He had shown the first man that he was different from all the animals. This was first demonstrated when God forbade him to eat the fruit of the tree, showing that Adam had a free will. God also brought the animals to Adam to be named, but after going through all of them, he realized that none of them were suitable companions for him because none had a reasoning soul. Adam was alone among all creation, and God, for the first time, saw that something was not good: "It is not good that the man should be alone" (Gen. 2:18). This was because one man, by himself, cannot represent and experience the fullness of what it means to be created as an image of God. God is a Trinity: His life, therefore, involves a communion of persons. God *is* a communion of persons.

For the image of God to be completed in man, therefore, he had to experience a communion of persons with one like himself. In something like a second or final creation, God made a woman out of Adam's rib. That Eve was formed from Adam's midsection, rather than his head or his foot, demonstrates that she is equal to him in this communion of persons. Adam recognizes her as one like himself, and he rejoices that he is not alone anymore.

John Paul II says that when Adam first saw Eve, he uttered the first great cry of joy in the history of the human race and spoke the first great wedding song. He who had named the animals and not found one like himself now names Eve and says: "This at last is bone of my bones and flesh of my flesh; she shall be called Woman, because she was taken out of Man" (Gen. 2:23). Eve allows herself to be recognized as one like him, and she rejoices, and the two form a unity of persons after the union of the Blessed Trinity. Their communion is complete and pure. It is a relationship of giving and receiving in love, not of domination or manipulation.

This is what it means when Scripture says that Adam and Eve were naked and not ashamed (Gen. 2:25). The shame and discomfort we feel about the naked body is not about the body itself, which is a good created by God. It was created by God, though, to be a medium through which the communion of persons in the heart would be expressed especially through sexuality and children. After the sin, though, we are exposed and vulnerable to manipulation—that the trust we express in revealing our full selves to another might be exploited. Clothing protects us physically, yes, but also emotionally and spiritually. In Adam and Eve's first relationship, there was no fear or distrust; they were both subjects of love, fully personal and fully free, together. Their sexuality was a seal or means by which they physically expressed an already existing union in their souls, which mirrored the communion of persons in the Trinity, of which it was an image.

Their union was also lasting and indissoluble, just as the persons of the Trinity never leave each other. When Christ was asked why Moses allowed writs of divorce, he replied, "For your hardness of heart Moses allowed you to divorce your wives, but from the beginning it was not so" (Matt. 19:8). "The beginning" refers to Genesis. It wasn't possible to dissolve the relationship of a man and a woman fully in union with one another and God because it would be like dissolving the Trinity.

Furthermore, just as the Trinity is life-giving, so is the marriage relationship. There's something divine about procreation: God directly participates in the bringing forth of new life by creating a soul. This, in fact, was one of the reasons women were purified after childbirth in the Old Testament. Like a chalice that, during Mass, comes into contact with the divine and must be purified, so did the woman, who had been part of a divine act by bringing forth a child. This procreative dimension, as we will see, must be affirmed in every marital act.

Sexual union is ordered to life, of course, but it stimulates a personal communion of love between the spouses after the manner of the Trinity. This is what we call the unitive dimension of marriage. The husband and wife must commit themselves to each other not as pleasure-seeking automatons but as real, vibrant, complete human persons. This unitive dimension is as important to the maintenance of marriage as the procreative dimension; both must go together, as they did in the marriage of Adam and Eve — until the first sin.

Fall from Grace

With the Original Sin, Adam and Eve questioned the gift of divine grace, and thus, their purity of intention was lost. This compromised their spousal love because the suspicion (and the reality) of manipulation entered their relationship. Their union was supposed to be an image of the Trinity, but when God was no longer present to them through grace, they lost the ability to give themselves in the complete and selfless manner of the Trinity. So, we read that they were naked *and* ashamed (see Gen. 3:7).

Adam became uneasy at the very presence of his body, and he and his wife no longer experienced the true spousal love of self-giving communion. They no longer completely trusted each other. They no longer experienced the fullness of peaceful intimacy. They no longer experienced the fact that sexuality does not exist to *cause* love, but to *express* love.

Marriage still existed with its original purpose, but now it was marred by the weakness and instrumentalization — the treating of one by another as a means to an end. John Paul II says that sex, from being a physical affirmation that "it is good that you exist," now became a statement that "you are good because you make me feel good." The Sixth Commandment recalls man to his original innocence. It affirms the necessity of marriage as a genuine communion of persons who share in the creative life of God. Each must be treated as a human person, respecting each other's rights and performing his own duties. Neither one can extort the gift of self—in sexuality or in other aspects of shared life—for his or her own gratification.

Pope John Paul II once said that it was possible for a husband to commit adultery with his wife, and this caused some surprise around the world. He said this in addressing the famous call of Christ in the Sermon on the Mount to return to a correct understanding of adultery as a sin of the manipulative heart:

> Adultery in the heart is committed not only because man looks in this way at a woman who is not his wife, but precisely because he looks at a woman in this way. Even if he looked in this way at the woman who is his wife, he could likewise commit adultery in his heart.[13]

The point is simply this: Just because a couple is married, it doesn't mean that anything goes. You do not sign away your dignity when you marry; rather, you are affirming that you will respect your spouse's dignity all the more. Procreation, therefore, goes together with the interpersonal dimension of marriage, the respect and freedom the spouses share and cultivate in each other. This way of looking at a woman, or vice versa, characterizes the state of Original Sin. But Christ does not accuse man or the body *as such*; rather, he wants to show that the body in shame is a body not sufficiently appreciated for what it was meant to be—and so now must be redeemed.

Return to Grace

The fullness of the experience of the body requires that it be redeemed and returned to its rightful place as a vehicle of the communion of

[13] John Paul II, *Theology of the Body*, 43, 2.

persons. Grace allows this to happen: "We know that the whole creation has been groaning in travail together until now; and not only the creation, but we ourselves, who have the first fruits of the Spirit, groan inwardly as we wait for adoption as sons, the redemption of our bodies" (Rom. 8:22–23). That very redemption requires returning human experience, by the healing power of grace, to a union of *eros* (the body and the passions) with *ethos* (the love and the will). This is done through the classic virtue of temperance: self-restraint born of love.

Again, this reflects the classic teaching of Saint Thomas: "In themselves passions are neither good nor evil. They are morally qualified only to the extent that they effectively engage reason and will.... It belongs to the perfection of the moral or human good that the passions be governed by reason."[14] This redemption forms the context of sacramental marriage.

Everything we have said so far pertains to natural marriage. It all has to do with our human nature, and everyone who commits himself to another in marriage takes on these responsibilities. But, in the New Law, marriage is also a sacrament of the New Testament. We now have the example of Christ pouring out His Blood on the Cross for the sake of His Spouse, the Church. We have an example from the God-Man of total fidelity—not just the communion of persons within the Trinity, but Christ's divine-and-human communion with the Church. And with that comes something the Old Law did not have: sacramental grace.

John Paul II expresses this whole doctrine of man and the relationship of marriage using both Ephesians 5:22–33 and the Song of Songs. He wishes to highlight that, according to Saint Paul in Ephesians, Christ seeks to recover the same value and meaning of

---

[14] CCC 1767, reflecting Saint Thomas Aquinas, *Summa Theologiae*, I-II, 24, 3.

marriage as spousal man experienced before the Fall—but now as expressing also His relationship with His Church, shown in His willingness to die for Her:

> *The institution of marriage* according to the words of Genesis 2:24, expresses not only the beginning of the fundamental human community, which by the "procreative" power proper to it ("be fruitful and multiply," Gen. 1:28) serves to continue the work of creation, but at the same time *it expresses the Creator's salvific initiative*, which corresponds to man's eternal election spoken about in Ephesians.[15]

The grace of marriage allows the parties to become one flesh, just as Christ is one with His Bride, the Church, and it calls forth from them the same love Christ has for His Church. This union is expressed when the spouses use their bodies to express their communion of souls in Christ and with each other. John Paul calls this the "language of the sign" or the "prophetism of the body." But there were both true and false prophets in the Old Testament, and so can the language of the body be true or false. For it to be true, it must reflect all the goods of marriage: fidelity (indissolubility), friendship (no manipulation), and fecundity (openness to life). This is the fullness of what marriage has to offer.

Some proponents of the Theology of the Body have made the strange logical jump from the fact the body is good and expresses this communion of hearts to the conclusion that by grace man returns to a kind of original justice in which he need not worry about the enticements of pleasures or concupiscence of the flesh. The pope is clear that one can never return to this state and that the condemnation of lust in Scripture is not about the body or the passions as such, but about the will. One can never act as though

---

[15] *Theology of the Body*, 506.

one is free from temptation in this life. Though spousal love can be an important part of the healing of our spirit in this regard, it does not do away with our weakness totally. "The 'hermeneutics of the sacrament' allows us to draw the conclusion that man is always *essentially 'called' and not merely 'accused,'* even inasmuch as he is precisely the 'man of concupiscence.'"[16] So a proper understanding of the body and marriage gives us hope — but not presumption.

Frustrating God's Plan

The Sixth Commandment specifically mentions adultery, which is a violation in justice of the union of persons implied in conjugal love. It is a kind of sacrilege in that it takes what is meant to be holy — the sexual union of husband and wife, participating with God in their own communion and, very often, in the creation of a new person — and treats it as a plaything. It is a kind of profanity in action.

The same pertains to divorce, as we have said. Now, merely obtaining a civil divorce is not an act of adultery. There can be times where such a step is necessary, or at least unavoidable. A person in such a tragic situation is still free to receive Communion and to participate in every way in the life of the Church. But to begin another sexual relationship without getting the first marriage annulled is adultery just as surely as any tawdry affair. And if one looks upon divorce as dissolving the union, then one does commit the sin of divorce. The *Catechism* states:

> *Divorce* is a grave offense against the natural law. It claims to break the contract, to which the spouses freely consented, to live with each other till death. Divorce does injury to

[16] Ibid., 547.

the covenant of salvation, of which sacramental marriage is the sign. Contracting a new union, even if it is recognized by civil law, adds to the gravity of the rupture: the remarried spouse is then in a situation of public and permanent adultery....

Divorce is immoral also because it introduces disorder into the family and into society. This disorder brings grave harm to the deserted spouse, to children traumatized by the separation of their parents and often torn between them, and because of its contagious effect which makes it truly a plague on society. (2384–2385)

There are some sins against this commandment, though, that are not directly addressed in it. Against the unitive dimension of marriage, there is rape, incest, and bestiality. Against the procreative dimension of marriage, we find birth control and sterilization. And against both dimensions, we find homosexuality and masturbation, because in these acts it is impossible either to procreate or to have a genuine union of persons.

Let us briefly consider these last two. Masturbation is using oneself as an *object* of pleasure, rather than seeing oneself as a *subject* of love. Is it any wonder we find so many people today who think their lives are worthless and meaningless? Masturbation conditions us to being objects of manipulation and use; it drains us of self-respect and recognition of our own dignity. We could say the same about homosexual acts, in which each person necessarily exploits the other for pleasure. Now, we must be clear that the mere *inclination* to homosexual acts is not sinful (though it is disordered). We mustn't judge the inclination or the person; indeed, we must instead do everything we can to help those who feel this inclination to appreciate their own dignity and what God wants for their relationships.

The Decalogue Decoded

Taking Control from God

Let's now examine the special problem of contraception, which we can define as excluding the possibility of having children by artificial means. This would also include acts of sterilization, such as vasectomies.

A couple does not have to expect to conceive in each conjugal act. During most of the fertility cycle, it is unlikely or impossible to conceive, and of course during pregnancy it is impossible to conceive: There's nothing wrong with enjoying the unitive quality of sexuality during these times. To actively work against procreation, however, by hijacking normal processes, either with physical barriers or with hormones, is to act against the very nature God has placed in sexuality. Thus, it is to act against our nature and dignity as persons made in His image.

Contraception is, in essence, an attempt to exclude the rights of the Creator in the marital relationship. Marriage images the Holy Trinity, and the Holy Trinity uses this relationship to bring forth other little images of the Trinity, and so He has a proprietorship here that must be respected. Just as we don't have absolute proprietorship of our own bodies (think of the impermissibility of suicide), so we do not have absolute proprietorship over sexuality. The spouses provide the material, but God alone provides the soul. The conjugal act, therefore, must express an interior attitude of fidelity not only between the spouses, but toward God.

Now, it is possible, through strictly natural means, to postpone having children, and the Church permits this, provided there is a just reason. Called Natural Family Planning (NFP), this lifestyle respects the Author of Nature, who has placed periods of natural infertility in our biology. Just reasons for postponing having children vary from family to family: They could involve finances or concerns of mental or physical health. The reason to postpone pregnancy cannot be, of course, simply a preference. Using NFP to postpone pregnancy must be a decision made in concert with God, thus respecting His rights in a couple's conjugal life.

In NFP, the natural order of the fertility God has placed in sexuality is affirmed, not denied. Further, NFP requires and fosters self-control during periods of abstinence; it requires that spouses work *with* their nature rather than *against* it. In turn, this advances their appreciation for the beauty of sexuality, as it becomes more special and less mundane. Thus, it preserves the nuptial meaning of the body.

The Church is not suspicious of the body as such. The flesh is not evil simply as flesh. Indeed, the body is good! After all, it's created by God. And so, sexuality is good. But all this must be placed in the proper order. If we exercise restraint with respect to the flesh, it can strengthen our reason and our will, putting even the most urgent passions of sexuality in their place. A sexuality under the authority of reason is not boring or staid, but all the more intimate, because spouses' bodies act in union with their souls in this most beautiful communion of persons.

Celibacy and Sexuality

Now, complete self-giving love need not be expressed only in and through marriage. This kind of love is always ordered toward the Trinity, but it doesn't have to be expressed in sexual relations. It is possible for a person to renounce the individual expression of this love between two persons for the sake of the Kingdom of Heaven. This is what we call celibacy.

Jesus said in the Gospel, "For there are eunuchs who have been so from birth, and there are eunuchs who have been made eunuchs by men, and there are eunuchs who have made themselves eunuchs for the sake of the kingdom of heaven" (Matt. 19:12). Here, Christ describes the conditions under which a person may seek to renounce completely the state of marriage in this life. No one may renounce the state of marriage simply out of fear of sexuality. Those who aren't yet married can have spousal love in its potential form for the person they hope to meet. People who are married, of course, enjoy spousal love in its fullness. Then there are the celibates, who renounce this state: They do so in order to show that one does not have to make love in order to be love. The Lord calls some people by an individual grace to renounce the state of marriage to one person, so that, like Mary and Joseph in their marriage, they may be married fully to Him and, in so doing, show what the Kingdom of Heaven is like.

In this way, those consecrated to celibacy encourage us all by showing that the Kingdom of Heaven, where we "neither marry nor are given in marriage, but are like angels," is not inhuman, but not fully human (Matt. 22:30). Further, they affirm the possibility and the beauty of bringing forth life through love in a spiritual way, not just a physical way. Thus, they remind us of the fullness of our human nature as physical and spiritual beings.

A person who embraces celibacy does not do so out of fear of fatherhood or motherhood. He or she wants very much to be a father or mother—but for an entire community rather than a family. This is a different and complementary kind of fatherhood or motherhood. Taken together, then, marriage and celibacy represent the fullness of the possibilities of self-giving and life-giving love. Abstinence from sexuality doesn't make a person cold, destructive, or indifferent. Rather, it opens up new horizons and opportunities for love in different ways.

This does not mean, of course, that everyone who feels called to celibacy is well adjusted and joyful. There are certainly many priests and religious who are frustrated, even deeply unhappy with their lives. This can happen for many reasons, just as with married and single laypeople, but one main factor is the lack of a deep personal prayer life. Without a committed prayer life, no one — married or celibate, lay or clergy — can fully understand and experience what self-giving love can be. This is especially dangerous for priests and other celibates, because they have so little to fall back on. Parents and other members of families have unavoidable relationships with others — especially needy and fussy children — who demand their attention and stimulate them to unselfish acts. But priests and religious have very little to keep them afloat spiritually if their prayer life suffers.

A Comprehensive Witness

Married people and those who embrace celibacy need a deep personal prayer life in order to discover and to embrace the freedom of chastity — that is, proper control of the sexual life according to one's state of life. Our relationship with God will encourage us to nourish and support those around us in the truth that the life of self-giving love is not just about sexuality and procreation, but about interpersonal communion. There is no worse argument for chastity than unhappy priests and religious. Frustrated celibates lead to frustrated married couples. On the other hand, there's no better argument for the fullness of earthly love — including the option for young people to consider a vocation to the priesthood or the religious life — than someone who has been given the grace by God to live the spousal life of virginity and is happy, integrated, and filled with life.

In regard to this commandment especially, we in the Church exist to aid and to support one another. For married couples, this means keeping the unitive and procreative aspects of sexuality in their proper union and letting God bring life out of their self-giving love in whatever way He chooses. And for priests and religious, that means demonstrating that love brings spiritual life into the world just as surely as physical life. Together, then, let us decide to enjoy and embrace the beautiful relationships of communion God has created us for, and thus to respect the reality of His life in us.

The Seventh Commandment

The Relationship between Man and Creation

The Seventh Commandment addresses injuries done to another person through the material goods necessary for the maintenance of bodily life. This is a genuine injury because we are body and soul together: Indeed, the body exists for the sake of the soul, and so we need material goods both for our bodies to thrive *and* to perfect our souls.

This commandment, which reads simply, "You shall not steal" (Exod. 20:15), principally forbids two actions: theft and robbery. Understanding these sins depends on understanding the necessity of material goods and on understanding why human beings have personal property to begin with.

When God created humanity, He said, "Let us make man in our image, after our likeness; and let them have dominion over the fish of the sea, and over the birds of the air, and over the cattle, and over all the earth, and over every creeping thing that creeps upon the earth." (Gen. 1:26). Man, therefore, is given specifically and directly by God dominion over the material world. This is part of what it means to be made in God's image: We act, in a sense, as His proxies here on earth, managing and distributing its goods (if we're doing it right) as He would—for the good of all. We do this using our most God-like feature, our rationality. When

Adam named all the animals, he showed that he was of a different character from all the other things God had made, and he assumed a kind of proprietorship over them. This gave him (and gives us) the natural right to use and to possess the material creation. But this right is proprietary.

So, we do not have an absolute dominion over creation, but rather a participatory dominion that recognizes that it was created by God and must be used according to His Law. We cannot decide for ourselves what is right and what is wrong with respect to creation; rather, we exercise our dominion as God's servants. Indeed, God imposed rules on our use of creation from the very beginning: "You may freely eat of every tree of the garden; but of the tree of the knowledge of good and evil you shall not eat" (Gen. 2:16–17). We use our reason to participate in God's final dominion over everything. We need material goods for the perfection of our souls, but we cannot on our own determine how those material goods are used, except in relationship to how they have been given to us by the all-loving Creator.

The Social Question

This brings us to the question of the use of material goods. We will end up spending most of this chapter on this question, because it is essential to understanding how this commandment applies to everyday circumstances. This is "the social question," and it refers to how goods and services are shared in the economic order. The central issues that have been discussed in and by the Church for centuries are the rights to private property and a just wage, which have their origins in the nature of work as it occurred before the Original Sin. As with adultery, one must go back to the beginning.

Human beings have always worked, because work simply is the application of the human, spiritual mind to the material order.

Work before the first sin, however, was not toilsome or burdensome. John Paul II says that the capacity for work does not come from the means of production but from the reasoning human mind. If there had been no Original Sin, and thus, no manipulation or selfishness, the remuneration for work, in the form of material goods, would have been shared by all according to their contribution and need. This is called the universal destination of goods, and we are still called to honor it today; it is necessary to understand the function of property and how it relates to social questions.

Ever since Leo XIII issued the first specifically social encyclical, *Rerum Novarum*, in 1891, in response to the problems created by the Industrial Revolution, there has been a great deal of misunderstanding about the Church's teaching concerning the economic order. Leo and later popes have mounted a two-front battle against materialist, capitalist, and socialist views of the social and economic order. Against capitalism, the popes have condemned not the simple taking of profit, but rather the idea that profit and wages should be entirely determined by the market, with no application of reason or considerations of the human needs and contributions of the workers.

The Church has also condemned the ideologies inspired by Karl Marx and his followers for the crass materialism they embraced just as surely as the most unrestrained capitalists did. The socialist attacks on property, in addition, misunderstood the very nature of man and his relationship with the material world. As we said, the idea of property is built into our nature as God's earthly proxies in the management of creation. But the necessity of property as a *social institution*, with the rules and regulations instituted by a civil authority, is a result of the Fall. Because of the Fall, the universal destination of goods has been perverted into greed based on manipulation. To preserve the right of each person to have what is needed for survival, human beings in general began to try to ensure that the basic needs of all would be provided for through the institution of property. Property became a right—but not an absolute one.

A Right to Property—But What Kind?

To understand the right to property, we must distinguish between two kinds of "natural" rights we have as human beings. The first are those we hold in common with the animals, things such as procreation and the rearing of offspring. These are parts of life that are simply implied in our biology and that it would be gravely unjust to frustrate. There are other natural rights, though, that we have to arrive at by contemplating what it means to live a fully human life, and what needs to be guaranteed to ensure that all of us have the ability to perfect our souls through our bodies. This is traditionally called the *jus gentium*, or "the right of nations," and property is this kind of natural right. There's nothing in the very nature of my toothbrush that makes it mine. We can say that property is "natural," though, in the sense that apportioning goods and land and so forth such that they can be cultivated and used for the common good of society is part of being human. Private property is a right but also entails a duty.

The possession of goods, therefore, must always be directed to the service of man—oneself or others. When we talk about one's own good, that includes the nurturing of one's family and the providing for the good of friends, dependents, and so on. The principal good, for example, of owning a factory is not only profit, but producing goods for the use of society and paying a just wage to workers. (The owner or developer of the factory may take a just profit for himself, in order to improve the product and to grow the company.) The law of property is not based on competition for the sake of profit, but on cooperation for the sake of serving man.

Private property, then, is the easiest and most perfect means for fallen men to ensure the disinterested development of material goods. The purpose of private productive property is that it be developed for the common good. As a result, property is a *relative*, not an *absolute*, right. As you can see, this militates against forms of socialism that would confiscate private property *and* against forms of capitalism that see the purpose of private property as producing private gains.

It is in the nature of property that those who labor on or with another's property will be justly compensated. The just wage has been defined by several popes as that which provides for the maintenance of the worker and his family in "becoming" conditions, assuming frugal and decent living. No matter what the labor is, the salary must at least reflect that it is a human person, not a machine, who does it. In this sense, one could say the Seventh Commandment flows directly from the Fifth, which has to do with respecting human life, and the Sixth, which has to do with preserving the life of the family. This may help us to understanding some teachings that are largely unknown and may be hard to comprehend.

For example, consider a man starving during a famine who comes upon surplus grain that someone is keeping to sell. If the owner charged exorbitant rates or had so little interest in feeding the hungry that he willed that those who could not pay should starve, it would *not* be a violation of the Seventh Commandment for the starving man to take some grain to preserve his life. In this case, the right of property is trumped by the universal destination of goods. We have a right to the things necessary for our survival, including and especially from the surplus of others. Similarly, the civil authority would be justified in expropriating the grain of surplus holders who attempt to profit in a crisis. Think of so many of our American ancestors who worked for little pay (or sometimes no pay at all). It would *not* violate the moral law for a cook who has been denied a just wage to take leftover food from her employers to feed her children.

We can see this reflected in the interpretation given to property rights in the Old Testament; these rights were real but were tempered by the law of firstfruits and the law of jubilees. See Deuteronomy 24:19: "When you reap your harvest in your field, and have forgotten a sheaf in the field, you shall not go back to get it; it shall be for the sojourner, the fatherless, and the widow; that the LORD your God may bless you in all the work of your hands." And in Leviticus, every fiftieth year involves debt cancellation, restoring the community and freedom, both marred by the bondage of debt. In fact, the American colonists chose Leviticus 25:10 for the Liberty Bell: "And you shall hallow the fiftieth year, and proclaim liberty throughout the land to all its inhabitants; it shall be a jubilee for you, when each of you shall return to his property and each of you shall return to his family."

Apostolic Poverty

Some people swear away their rights to property to live a more ascetic life, such as members of mendicant orders or other monks and nuns. This is a special grace from God that allows for a more complete, apostolic sharing of life that has its origin in the Acts of the Apostles and in the admonition of the Lord to the rich young man: "If you would be perfect, go, sell what you possess and give to the poor, and you will have treasure in heaven; and come, follow me" (Matt. 19:21).

To be clear, this is not some kind of socialism. In doctrinaire Marxism, man becomes an instrument of matter; his destiny is said to be determined by his material situation. The relation of workers to employers is one of warfare and competition for power; distributive justice on the Marxist account is to redistribute wealth forcibly based on someone's conception of social engineering. But in a genuine vow of poverty, one voluntarily renounces the certainty of ownership for the sake of using material goods for the perfection of the Spirit. Matter serves man.

Labor and Wages in Catholic Social Teaching

When we deny the right to a just wage, though, and depend entirely on the guidance of "the market" for prices for labor, we make the same mistake as the Marxists, placing man at the service of mammon. But the motive of having and developing private property is not meant to be profit, which obeys some fatalistic, supposedly natural law of supply and demand, as the liberal capitalists thought, but the perfection of the self and others. The work of the genuine capitalist is one of justice and love toward the neighbor, both in producing helpful goods and services and in supporting employees and their families. Real capital exists to serve society by providing a good product, just wages, employment, and development of the common good.

Labor, that is, is not a commodity just to be bought and sold. It is a true expression of a human being's rational faculties, a true part of us. The just wage is an obligation to treat the worker as a human being, not just another economic input.

When Pope Leo XIII wrote the primordial social encyclical, he sought to address both Marxism and unbridled capitalism, charting a middle course between the two. He denied the laissez-faire capitalism of the nineteenth century, in which economics was based strictly on the deterministic "law" of supply and demand. He also affirmed that, while the state could make laws about property and business, it could play only a supplementary role in managing these affairs. For instance, the state could nationalize an industry, such as the railroads, in a time of emergency, as during a war — but when the emergency passed, ownership had to be returned to the private sector.

Leo enumerated the duties of workers to their employers to complete a just day's work, but he also demanded a salary that reflect the demands of dignity. Wages for work were thus declared to be a moral and human question, and not simply matters of markets and negotiations. The pope also condemned class struggle as unnatural, but recognized the rights of workers to organize unions, even if these excluded employers. The tactic of the strike is also implicitly recognized, though two principles must be fulfilled for it to be morally good: It must be nonviolent, and it must not be an expression of class warfare. In other words, the final purpose of the strike must be to encourage employers to act justly, not simply to defeat them.

Later popes have developed these social ideals further. At first, labor unions were only tolerated, and Catholics were encouraged to join only Catholic unions, but in *Quadragesimo Anno* (1931), Pius XI approved nonconfessional unions. He defended the guild system concept, which was protectionist and united employers and workers in a common cause, but he also affirmed that workers could actively defend their rights in order to guarantee a just wage. In a further repudiation of Marx, Pius echoed Leo's condemnation of class struggle. In response to the growing dangers of the early 1930s, he warned against centralization of economic power, either in monopolies or in the state, a rebuke of Fascist and Nazi total regimes.

In the postwar era, Saint John XXIII's *Mater et Magistra* (1961) encouraged state intervention for a just and prosperous economy, but not the substitution of the state for the private sector. Paul VI also taught in *Populorum Progressio* (1967) that the social question could no longer be localized in individual states but must be considered in an international context. World peace demanded that all the nations embrace some level of state cooperation and that individual societies recognize that what affects one always affects others.

When it comes specifically to the question of labor, John Paul II's *Laborem Exercens* (1981) is the fullest examination of the matter. The pope specifically states that labor (the multitude of people who lack productive property) is prior to capital (the small but highly influential group of entrepreneurs, owners, and holders of the means of production). John Paul II points out that in the beginning of the Industrial Revolution, capital not only became separated from labor but was viewed in opposition to it. This led to a hardening of positions, and the dignity and true purpose of work — that is, the application of the spiritual mind to God's creation and the building up of the common good — were left out of the picture. This, in turn, fostered the twin errors of "economism" (the idea of human labor solely as an economic commodity), which is based on the emphasis of a materialistic philosophy that does not include the soul, and "collectivism" (the idea that human labor has no personal dimension at all).

Though the anti-personal Marxist collective solution and denial of private property cannot be embraced, neither can an exaggerated capitalism. The pope evokes Thomas Aquinas in two instances to correct these notions. First, capital is not naturally in opposition to labor but "should serve labor, and thus, by serving labor, ... should make possible the achievement of the first principle of this order, namely, the universal destination of goods and the right of common use of them."[17] Second, "the Church's teaching has always expressed the strong and deep conviction that man's work concerns not only the economy but also, and especially, personal values.... This is the principal reason in favor of the private ownership of the means of production."[18]

[17] Pope John Paul II, *Laborem Exercens* (September 14, 1981), no. 14.
[18] Ibid., no. 15.

As for the rights of workers, John Paul II argues that the state is a kind of "indirect employer" who has more responsibility for wages and other aspects of the business relationship. Maximizing profit cannot be the only goal of business. Since all property has a human dimension, "the objective rights of the worker ... must constitute the adequate and fundamental criterion for shaping the whole economy."[19] John Paul II reaffirms former papal teaching that a just wage is the family wage, which he defines as follows: "a single salary given to the head of the family for his work, sufficient for the needs of the family without the other spouse having to take up gainful employment outside the home."[20]

The conscience of the entrepreneur is the essential place in where the balancing of goods, with the worker at the forefront, is supposed to occur. In particular, the Christian entrepreneur is asked to apply the gospel always to the reality in which he operates — and the gospel asks him to put in the first place the human person and the common good. His first duty is to provide fitting and justly compensated work. The Christian businessman is to collaborate with others who share his conviction and to seek to widen the network of just and humane business as much as possible.[21]

This is the sense of the call of Pope Francis for redistribution of wealth. This is not to be understood as a kind of government-mandated socialism that takes profits from companies and practices widespread state ownership simply to distribute free checks. It is rather a realistic attempt to introduce into the economy the fact that work is not an end and that man is not a utilitarian means to profit. Francis's emphases are in the great tradition of the Church's

---

[19] Ibid., no. 17.

[20] Ibid., no. 19.

[21] See Pope Francis, Address to the *Centesimus Annus Pro Pontifice* Foundation (May 14, 2014).

teaching that there is a social duty that goes along with wealth. It is a denial of materialism and a focus on the spiritual character of human work.

Theft and Robbery

Now we must return to the distinction between the sins of theft and robbery. Theft, strictly speaking, is an unjust taking by stealth; to take by force or coercion is robbery. The sin of theft is strictly contrary to the precept of justice, that each person has dominion over the material he needs to fulfill the duties of his state in life. Thus, theft is not an attack on the material itself, but on the owner, even if no violence occurs.

The obvious examples of robbery are muggings, piracy, and other such assaults. But it's possible to act against the material livelihood of another by sins of omission. For instance, the refusal to pay a just wage is a sin of omission and is the same as robbery — especially because it almost always includes coercion in the form of implied threats of unemployment or worse. The refusal to give to the poor from a person's surplus, according to the unanimous opinion of the Church Fathers, is also a kind of robbery. A person has a right to survival. Saint Basil said pointedly, "It is the hungry man's bread you withhold. It is the naked man's cloak you store away."[22]

Sins against the Seventh Commandment do not always involve burglary or violence or open theft. All kinds of robberies are committed by people with perfect grooming and French cuffs in skyscraper offices. Unjust prices, unjust wages, unjust buying, and unjust selling are all examples of robbery. Consider the Old Testament's approach to the possession of material goods. The right to property is certainly affirmed; the owner may take the first yield of

[22] Saint Basil, Homily on Luke 12:18.

the harvest. But the second and third yields belong to the widows, the orphans, and the strangers. This isn't a charitable suggestion; it's a duty of justice. This is humanity; it is the way human economics ought to operate.

Sins against this commandment can, of course, be either mortal or venial. It depends on what is taken and from whom and in what circumstances: To take fifty dollars from a millionaire is probably a venial sin; to take fifty dollars from a poor widow is almost certainly a mortal sin. An overdraft fee leveled on the poor might be more evil than the acts of a pickpocket.

For all these sins, the proper moral response is restitution, which restores the balance of equity. This is specifically seen in the justice among equals called "commutative justice." A person has no right to retain what belongs to another. When it is impossible to restore precisely the thing taken, the person must restore to the owner something equivalent in value, as far as possible. (This extends from physical property to a person's good name, or any other good we can think of.) Normally, it suffices to restore the exact amount or thing, but if the money has been used to make a capital investment, the original owner has a right to gains on what was stolen. And if the theft or robbery has involved violence, then more than the amount must be restored, up to and including a prison sentence. Restitution must be made to the person himself, or if this is impossible, to the person's heirs; if all this is impossible, the offender may make restitution by good works, but he cannot keep money or goods obtained unjustly. Restitution should be made as soon as possible. One must remember that, in Scripture, the laborer is paid at the end of the day.

A Dignified Economics

The Seventh Commandment addresses the material goods and circumstances that are, in a sense, extensions of a person's soul.

It protects the material well-being that is essential for spiritual flourishing. The act of theft, then, is an act directly against the personhood of another, and thus against an image of God. But not all taking is theft, and not all theft involves taking: One can steal from another by not giving him his due, by not treating him as a human being in the workplace, by charging unjust prices, or by scheming to get an unjust yield. What the Seventh Commandment demands of us is an economic and political order in which we treat everyone as an image of God.

The Eighth Commandment

Words that Wound

After several commandments that address deeds, we will now discuss words that can wound. The Epistle of James compares the tongue to a ship's rudder: a small part that steers the whole, for good or for ill (James 3:1–5). If we fail to gain control over our words, we will struggle to gain control over the rest of our actions. There are many sins one must avoid in order to live with integrity in the truth.

Law and Order

First, there are virtues and sins that directly relate to what the Eighth Commandment addresses: speech in a court of law. "You shall not bear false witness against your neighbor" (Exod. 20:16). This refers not only to a witness giving testimony but to any officer of the court—a judge or attorney or party to the case—who fails to carry out his duty justly. The first person this commandment touches is the man or woman in charge of the courtroom, the judge. The judge must be just.

A judge is obligated to see that justice is done in the cases before him, and that requires that he follow the laws he administers. So, it would be a violation of this commandment for a judge to try a case over which he has no jurisdiction. He must make his judgments based on the evidence presented, not on other personal knowledge or biases. He represents not himself, but the civil law itself, which is ordered toward the common good of the community. This means he must follow the law when it comes to sentencing, but mercy may be applied, for the common good, when prudent.

Judges must pass sentence only on those who come under their jurisdiction, and that judgment must be passed only according to the rules of evidence. Even were the judge to have private knowledge that a defendant is guilty, he could not base his judgment on that. If he does have private knowledge, he can use it to guide himself in reexamining a case when he sees that an injustice may have been done for lack of evidence. No judgment can be passed on someone who is not formally accused because the office of the judge is to determine the rights of people and to interpret these rights between accused and accuser; he cannot bring charges himself. A judge may morally exercise mercy in those areas that lie within his power of discretion and where the sentence is not determined by law.

Now, in order for there to be a case to judge, a formal accusation must be made, and these accusations can violate the Eighth Commandment in a special way. An accusation must be made for the sake of the good of the accused—for his amendment—not out of malice or spite. A person who knows firsthand (not through hearsay) of a crime, though, is obliged to accuse—provided there is sufficient evidence. One may usually still accuse with direct knowledge but without further proof, but is less obliged to do so.

Every human society has developed ways of managing the difficulty caused by people who make accusations carelessly. It is not just personally but socially damaging for accusations to be made willy-nilly. Therefore, any accusation that is made in accord with the Eighth Commandment must be made in writing and signed: One must commit one's name to the charge. Saint Thomas Aquinas, in fact, taught that it is sinful for one to accuse a person of a crime when one can't prove the accusation because it unjustly puts the person in danger. The careless accuser, according to Thomas, should be himself charged with a crime.

The accused, of course, also has duties under this commandment. Modern rules of evidence have affected the implementation of the duties of the accused, so let's begin with his rights. First, he has a right to carry on a just defense. An accused is presumed innocent until proven guilty. A "not guilty" plea is not an affirmation of innocence, but rather an affirmation that the burden of proof is on the court according to the rules of evidence. Every accused person must know who accused him and what the charge is.

If the accused submits to direct examination, however, he must tell the truth about himself. The accused may licitly evade questions that are not material to the accusation, but he may never tell an intentional falsehood under oath. The accused may also not seek to discredit the accuser through slander or gossip. After the trial, a convicted person who knows that he has been judged and sentenced fairly may not appeal his case. To do so would be a kind of deceit that violates the Eighth Commandment—not to mention clogging up the court system. Generally speaking, the classical teaching in moral theology has been that a person who is justly condemned must submit peacefully to his punishment. If his punishment is not just, however, he may evade it through legal appeal or even escape from jail. He can frighten the guards, but not harm them.

As for the witnesses in court, it is the duty of a person to give testimony if he is called to do so. Moreover, if a person knows his testimony will prevent a serious miscarriage of justice, he has a specific obligation to come forward and offer his testimony. On the other hand, to lie under oath is the grave sin of perjury, of course, as we discussed in the Second Commandment. Even if a person tells a lie in only a trivial matter when he is on the witness stand, he has still committed a mortal sin because he has asked God, the First Truth, to bear witness to what he has said.

As to lawyers, justice demands that they defend the poor if the accused would not have legal counsel otherwise. In a criminal case, a defense lawyer may refuse unless he is the only person who can mount a defense. The lawyer is morally obliged to remain competent in his field and is also bound in justice to read and study the brief and not to take work he cannot competently perform. A lawyer cannot knowingly defend an accused he knows is guilty *by direct knowledge*. He must use only just means in mounting his case; he cannot use false evidence or, of course, lie. Some television shows and stereotypes might make the lawyerly profession sound like an "anything goes" Wild West of truthfulness, but traditionally this is the field where the truth is most valued and most important.

Words as Weapons: Five Ways

Though the Eighth Commandment might refer directly to courts of law, it also has important applications to everyday life. Sinful speech (outside of outright lying, which we will consider later) can be divided into five main categories: reviling, backbiting, whispering, derision, and cursing. In ordinary discourse, we owe each other in justice a certain honor and generosity as images of God. This is seriously compromised, however, by injurious words, which can destroy things that are more precious to others than even their material possessions — such as their reputations. These words betray an interior disposition that desires the destruction of another person.

To revile is to use speech to attack another person openly for the purpose of robbing him of his good name. This sin is ordered against the good of another human being, especially in grave matters, because it attacks something at the very heart of his identity and standing in society. Now, it is possible to speak bluntly to another person about his faults in a licit, even good way: to correct him out of genuine concern for his good. But to attack a person's good name intentionally for the purpose of injuring him is always wrong.

Sometimes, however, for the sake of other people, justice may require that we *submit* to being reviled. This is a good example of Jesus' teaching to "turn the other cheek." This doesn't mean that we should retreat into passivity and victimhood; rather, there may be times when to answer an attack would do more harm to others and to the common good than quietly bearing it. Think also of the spiritual work of mercy "to bear wrongs patiently." If we must answer back, we should feel no scruples about it, but our response must be ordered to the good of the reviler or the common good; it can't be only about justifying ourselves.

A companion sin to reviling is backbiting. Whereas the former is done openly, the latter is done in secret. Backbiting is when a person tries to injure another's good name by spreading stories about him—even true stories or bits of information—in order to hurt his reputation. If this is done through lies, it is known as calumny or scandal. If it is done with harmful and unnecessary spreading of truth, it is known as detraction.

It is easy to convince ourselves there is nothing wrong about talking about others behind their backs as long as what is said is true. "He really did do that awful thing," we tell ourselves. But it is just as wrong to destroy a person's good name among friends as among strangers. Everyone has a right to the protection of his good name; we are not always obliged to tell everyone everything that we know about others. Backbiting can be morally sinful character assassination just as surely as telling lies. In fact, backbiting can be a more grievous sin than theft because reputations can be more valuable — and certainly harder to replace — than material goods. We should note, though, that there can be good reasons to speak of another's faults to a third party, such as warning a friend about to enter a relationship. If damaging truths are spoken out of concern for the good of all involved, it is not backbiting.

The next sin is called whispering, which is a traditional term for what we would call gossip. When we whisper against someone, we rouse others against him. This sin is worse than backbiting because it targets the friends and other connections of the person in question to turn them against him. It is a kind of sabotage or vandalism of relationships. It is deeply antisocial, attacking the very heart of genuine human communities: friendship. No one can live a fully human life without friends. Indeed, the more friends we have, the more we wish to share love and friendship with others. Someone who intentionally sets out to destroy a person's friendships attacks not only that person as an individual but also the entire community.

This brings us to derision, which has to do with making fun of other people. Of course, there's a certain kind of humorous cama-raderie that's venially sinful at most — though we must be aware of our inner disposition toward the person, so that we are not hiding our scorn in "jokes." But to intentionally bring shame to someone through laughter or embarrassment in order to hurt that person is a very serious sin.

There is a great story about Saint Thomas Aquinas, who was apparently very guileless, especially in his youth. His fellow seminar-ians used to call him the "dumb ox." One day, it is said, his peers, in order to watch and deride his reaction, told him that a cow was flying outside the window. Now, of course, Thomas Aquinas was such a student of nature that it would have been impossible for him to think that this was happening. Nonetheless, he went to the window and looked out, and they all laughed at how stupid he was. Then he turned around and said to them, "Well, brothers,

I'd rather believe that a cow could fly than that my brother could lie to me." And that was the end of that.

The final personal sin against this commandment is cursing, in which we seek to invoke evil upon another person. Not every invocation of evil is against the Eighth Commandment: For instance, the Church does not sin when She declares an anathema. And usually when we "curse" someone else, we do not actually desire that our words be fulfilled; this is careless and vain speech, perhaps against the Second Commandment if we use the Lord's Name, but it is not necessarily mortally sinful. Cursing is a grave sin, however, when a person does mean it, when he really desires that some evil befall another person. It is not, however, as grave as backbiting, because backbiting does injury, whereas cursing only wishes it to be done. Cussing is usually merely impolite speech and can become a sin depending on how much scandal it causes. Normally it is of slight matter, though.

To Tell the Truth

And then there is lying. To lie, the *Catechism* states, is "to speak or act against the truth to lead someone into error" (2483). Truth has objective rights; error has no rights. The level of intention to lead another into error may affect one's culpability in lying, but it does not affect the objective immorality of the act itself.

It is interesting, however, that the original edition of the *Catechism* included the qualification that a lie was to deceive "someone who has a right to know the truth." This was later dropped in the official Latin edition and placed in a later part of the volume. This concept remains, though, an important aspect of thinking critically about deceit. For example, Church officials falsified baptismal records during World War II to save Jews from Nazi extermination. It would seem that this was not lying, even though the paper was false, because the Nazi regime had no right to know who is baptized legally. The *Catechism* states:

> Charity and respect for the truth dictate the response to every request for information or communication. The good and safety of others, respect for privacy, and the common good are sufficient reasons for being silent about what ought to not be known or for making use of discreet language.... No one is bound to reveal the truth to someone who does not have a right to know it. (2489)

The gravity of lying depends on the nature of the truth involved. Simply lying to a door-to-door salesman about whether your mother is home is at most a venial sin. Still, one should never underestimate the problem of lying, for people can quickly become accustomed to it. The more people lie, especially those in authority, the less freedom and trust can exist in the human community.

The duty to tell the truth is especially incumbent on authorities and those who present public information. To lie in the news media is an especially grievous sin. Those entrusted with information for the public good, whether in government or the media, have a grave moral obligation to tell the truth, including, for instance, not proclaiming others to be guilty of crimes without sufficient evidence.

Also included in this commandment is the necessity of preserving secrets. There are many kinds of secrets, from the personally entrusted secret to the professional secret to the most sacred of all, the seal of confession. The moral obligation to preserve a secret is not unconditional: In some situations, it may seriously harm the common good to preserve a secret, even a professional one. Professional secrets are primarily meant to ensure truthful communication between the professional and his client or potential clients. In a case of impending serious violence, for instance, the professional, out of both justice and charity, is bound to reveal secrets for the sake of the common good.

This is not the case with the seal of confession, which is entirely inviolable. The seal respects words spoken between the soul and Christ; the priest is merely the human, visible mediator of a dialogue that occurs between the private individual conscience and Christ. In justice, he has no right to reveal any part of that dialogue, as it is not his to reveal. The Church must resist any attempt to interfere in this most sacred communication. The *Catechism* is clear: "The secret of the sacrament of reconciliation is sacred and cannot be violated under any pretext. 'The sacramental seal is inviolable; therefore, it is a crime for a confessor to in any way betray a penitent by word or in any other manner or for any reason'"[23] (2490).

Lies committed by those entrusted with the truth take on the added weight of scandal. There is active and passive scandal. Active scandal is when a person commits a sin that leads another astray. For instance, if clerics lie about the Church or if the government lies about laws, then trust in these essential institutions is corroded. Passive scandal, on the other hand, results from someone who is looking for occasions to be scandalized even from good works. An example would be the Pharisees who claimed that Christ cast out demons by means of demons. Here the fault is on them: They ginned up a scandal when one did not actually exist. The dignity of the person who lies can give special weight to the evil of the lie, as more authoritative lies introduce more disorder into society and the Church.

We must take our speech seriously: It is easier than we often realize to wound the personhood of another. Let us, therefore, guard our speech and speak, as Saint Paul says, "only such as is good for edifying, as fits the occasion, that it may impart grace to those who hear" (Eph. 4:29).

[23] *Code of Canon Law*, 983, no. 1.

The Ninth and Tenth Commandments

Hearts and Minds

And now we turn to the final two commandments, which address covetousness: "You shall not covet your neighbor's house; you shall not covet your neighbor's wife, or his manservant, or his maidservant, or his ox, or his ass, or anything that is your neighbor's" (Exod. 20:17). These are usually separated into coveting *persons* and *things*.

The Divine Law of God is like the human law in that it is an ordinance of reason that directs our conduct. But it diverges from human law in that it also seeks to direct something only God can see: our hearts. These commandments have to do with the intention and disposition that underlie and often anticipate our actions.

What does it mean to covet in this context? It is based on the weakness we inherit from Original Sin, which is described by Saint Augustine as the "desire to dominate" and to manipulate others. The traditional word used for this is *concupiscence*. Those who refuse to find their fulfillment in God seek power by using something else as a substitute for God.

Temperance and Lust

These last two commandments are about the virtue of temperance, which has to do with reining in the passions. Weakness in this regard can lead us to act as if pleasure is the only good, at the expense of justice and charity. The commandments address the celebrated three lusts inherited from the Old Testament: "For all that is in the world, the lust of the flesh and the lust of the eyes and the pride of life, is not of the Father but is of the world" (1 John 2:16).

This is clearly seen by considering covetousness toward others' goods—the lust of the eyes. Sins in thought are less grave than sins in word or in deed, but they are often the beginning of an act of sin. These sins of thought range from idle jealousy to deep consideration that one would act on if only the chance arose and finally to planning and executing an act against another person's goods or reputation.

We covet others' material possessions because we seek fulfill-ment in lower goods as opposed to higher goods. This desire for lower goods often leads to envy and anger, which can lead to further sins and antisocial behavior. Envy and anger feed a spirit of pos-sessiveness that bleeds into the culture, which, in turn, influences others. What else is consumerism but the attempt to inspire pos-sessiveness that others can capitalize on?

This interior covetousness leads us to act against justice—the equitable (not equal) distribution of goods in the community—and liberality—the spirit of generosity and detachment by which we share freely and joyfully with others. Covetousness leads to rest-lessness as we mull over our insatiable desire to possess; it robs us of peace of mind.

This soon comes to define not just individual psyches, but an entire culture, as our obsession with consumerism demon-strates. This comes from and contributes to a kind of spiritual bankruptcy—a lack of union with and enjoyment of God. In a kind of religious conversion, we adhere to material things instead of God.

The Ninth and Tenth Commandments

The Role of the Passions

Let's consider the nature of the passions themselves. Though our greed blinds us to the truth and can be motivated by pleasure, pain, hope, and fear for our material lives, the passions themselves are not the problem. The participation of the passions in moral acts is, in fact, necessary because man is, by nature, still an animal. The passions, as part of that nature, form a kind of middle ground between the spirit and the body; thus, they participate in both realms. Though they are never the central issue in choice — that is, the will — they are present in every person and in every act because a movement in the higher part of the soul must be accompanied by a movement in the lower part. Well-formed passions, therefore, support spontaneity in good choices, while ill-formed passions support spontaneity in evil choices.

According to Aristotle there are eleven passions, most of which are enumerated in the *Catechism*. There was a long debate in the early Church caused by the influence of the philosophy of Stoicism regarding the place of the passions in morals. This has returned to the forefront today by the modern emphasis on the passions as areas of moral concern and, some would even say, wisdom. We can summarize the controversy by considering two contrary and extreme schools of thought.

The Stoic-influenced school maintained that the passions were sicknesses of the soul. They interfered with human freedom and were the principle cause of human beings acting contrary to their nature, and so they were considered to be evil in themselves. The best way to become virtuous, on the Stoic account, was to become completely dispassionate. A perfect human being was one who was cold, aloof, and entirely logical.

On the other hand, there is the "if it feels good, do it" ethos of modern life, which holds that the passions should be given totally free reign. Anything else, the idea goes, is somehow inauthentic, even psychologically dangerous.

The answer, of course, is in between. The life of virtue involves the passions because they are good in themselves, created by God for a reason. One who cannot feel anger, for instance, is easily victimized by evil. Sorrow comes with the perception of an evil and can be a powerful motivation to remove sin. Because the passions are present in the immortal soul, which includes biological and spiritual powers, they must be guided in self-restraining love by the intellect and the will. This means that they must neither be killed off nor indulged with complete abandon. "It belongs to the perfection of the moral or human good that the passions be governed by reason."[24] This leads to a real difference in the way the intellect and will govern the members of the body and the passions. The members of the body have no knowing or desiring power, and so they cannot resist the command of the intellect and the will. But the passions have sense knowledge and can desire sense input, and so they can resist the commands of reason.

> Hence, Aristotle says in the *Politics* that the soul rules the body as a despot would, as a master rules a slave who does not have the capacity to resist the master's command. But reason rules the interior parts of the soul by a royal and political governance, that is, as kings and princes rule free men who have the right and capacity to resist to some degree the commands of the king or prince.[25]

The passions are therefore neither moral nor immoral as such. They are always present in the psyche, and since they have an affective life of their own, they are taken up into the virtues and can make virtuous acts more spontaneous. On the other hand, they can also further pervert the vices, making them even more freely desired.

---

[24] Saint Thomas Aquinas, *Summa Theologiae*, I-II, 24, 3.
[25] Saint Thomas Aquinas, *On the Virtues in General*, 1, 4 ad corp.

Since the Original Sin, the passions tend to arise in us before reason can be brought to bear, and thus, they color our judgment. It is precisely for this reason that the formation of the passions is so essential to living virtuously. When the appetites—another word for the passions—are not suppressed, but rather trained to participate in the reasonable good, there is peace in the character as we truly enjoy doing the good more freely. Reason and the passions are not necessarily opposed; they were made, in fact, to support one another.

Mine!

When it comes to the lust of the eyes, there is nothing wrong with the material goods or riches in themselves. But since the Original Sin, our possessiveness always threatens to take over, and if indulged, it becomes insatiable. As noted in our discussion of the Seventh Commandment, the original meaning of work was the universal destination of human goods. In the state of infused contemplation, man did not seek to say "mine" of anything. The goods of creation are destined for the whole human race.... The universal destination of goods remains primordial, even if the promotion of the common good requires respect for the right to private property and its exercise" (CCC 2402–2403). This universal use is based on free exchange among persons dedicated to each other's good and is necessary for the perfection of the domestic and economic orders.

With sin, all of this changes. Without grace, the human race cannot arrive at the union with God that alone can satisfy the human soul. Other goods and desires are substituted for God, and they cannot possibly give the same satisfaction. Human beings try to control those things that they perceive can bring them happiness, satisfaction, and even perfection. When we have the grace of God, we need only the minimum to survive in this world, enough to have a decent quality of life. When we find our joy in Him, we do not have to search restlessly for things to possess or power to accumulate.

Adultery in the Heart

Coveting another's wife is lust of the flesh. Concupiscence is not simply a product of the body or the emotions. No matter what people might say about Catholicism, the Church does not hold the body or the emotions to be bad! Everything about mankind was made to be good by God, Who is goodness itself. At the beginning, all the powers of man were in a marvelous unity, ordered by God in holiness and justice. There was no concupiscence, no lust, no manipulation. The body served the emotions, and the emotions served the intellect and the will. This includes attraction and pleasure.

Saint Thomas Aquinas held, in fact, that not only did Adam and Eve have sex in paradise; they experienced more pleasure than people do now. But, importantly, it was not a pleasure that led to manipulation, because their emotions were perfectly and spontaneously at the service of their higher character, guarded by the grace of God. Indeed, it was God Himself Who placed pleasure in sex, just as He placed pleasure in eating: Both are essential to life.

After the Fall, as we have said, the relationship between Adam and Eve changed. They lost interior integrity and wanted to play by their own rules. They became alienated from themselves and from their world because they had become alienated from God. The pleasure of sex remained, but now it became an occasion of weakness that led them to use one another for manipulation and even domination. God said to Eve, "Your desire shall be for your husband, and he shall rule over you" (Gen. 3:16). Covetousness is caused by the loss of the presence of God.

All the powers God gave to humanity—the intellect, the will, the emotions, the body—have gone their own way since the Fall:

Under Original Sin, people became like a rebellious city, and the rebellion was passed down the generations. Cain slew Abel out of jealousy. The family was fractured. The character of the human heart went both deeper and outward, further corrupting the soul and society and even language. The Tower of Babel, which should have been the sign of our unity, became the very sign of our alienation from each other. All of this was due to a loss of interior union with God.

Jesus addressed the corrosive power of lust and covetousness when He said, "But I say to you that every one who looks at a woman lustfully has already committed adultery with her in his heart" (Matt. 5:28). This does not, of course, refer to any glance at a member of the opposite sex: It refers to an attitude of soul whereby we look at others with an eye toward how to manipulate them especially for the sake of pleasure. This is a serious personal disorder for one created in the image of God. As we mentioned when discussing the Sixth Commandment, it's also possible to reduce one's spouse to an object of lust, regarding him or her as an object of pleasure to manipulate.

Harnessing the Passions

How does the Law of God seek to remedy these disordered desires? The first remedy is a commonsense one: Avoid situations where these desires tend to arise. Don't go to places or watch entertainment that's intended to provoke lust if you don't want to feel lust! It's so much easier to avoid disordered desires when we avoid the predictable precursors to those desires. This is especially true today of Internet pornography. Turn from the computer, perhaps pray before using it, and have devotional objects nearby so that when you are tempted, you can distract yourself. Identify a good hobby or another action you enjoy, and pick that up when you are tempted to enjoy something evil. Sins with the body begin with desires in the heart and with fantasies that are not addressed and are allowed to run amok.

Second, perform works of penance to tame the desires of the heart. The body and the emotions and pleasure itself are not evil; they are simply ways we can experience evil. We choose evil with our will, and our will can be trained with respect to those temptations and triggers that it struggles with the most. We do not practice mortification of our desires because they are in themselves wrong, but because having control over them is good. A person becomes a victim of his passions because of a weakness in his will. A will guided by reason must be the cornerstone of all genuine human freedom.

If you practice physical penances, remember that these are essentially *symbols* of penance, not penance itself, which requires elevating and entrusted our suffering to the Lord. Furthermore, never take on a physical penance without the advice of a confessor.

And third, pray assiduously. After all, Adam committed his Original Sin by failing to attend to God, by failing to act and to ask for His grace. Adam had to pray continually in order to preserve the condition of integrity with which he was created, and the same is true for us. We must attend to the Trinity for all that is good and true, and this is especially important in trying to control lust within us. We can also be sure to pursue wholesome hobbies and other endeavors, such as investigating Divine Truth through spiritual reading.

All this talk about lust and concupiscence and commandments seems quaint in our modern world, but it's precisely because there is something divine about human life, about human destiny, and about the human body that we must take this topic to heart. Chastity is not about a list of prohibitions, but about living a fully human life that respects and reaches for that divinity. Chastity is a safeguard against the corruption of love by the disordered and depersonalized experience of pleasure that ignores the rights and dignity of the Creator. It is about integrity: the union of feeling and reason and will and body in Christ.

The Code Cracked: Rediscovering Our Dignity

These reflections on the Ten Commandments have been about rediscovering the image of God in man — *in you*. How sad, how degraded, how corrupted we have made ourselves by not taking these Commandments seriously. In the guise of autonomy and individuality, people today fail to attend to the action of the Holy Spirit. But the presence of the Holy Spirit is power itself, and our attention to Him is necessary for us to live this life to the fullest.

The Ten Commandments offer us nothing less than the code to unlocking the full potential of our humanity by restoring the integrity of all the powers God has given us. Deuteronomy says it best:

> See, I have set before you this day life and good, death and evil. If you obey the commandments of the LORD your God which I command you this day, by loving the LORD your God, by walking in his ways, and by keeping his commandments and his statutes and his ordinances, then you shall live and multiply. (30:15–16)

So choose life!

About the Author

Fr. Brian Thomas Becket Mullady is the son of an Air Force officer and was raised throughout the United States. He entered the Dominican Order in 1966 and was ordained in Oakland, California, in 1972. He has been a parish priest, high school teacher, retreat master, mission preacher, and university professor. He received his doctorate in sacred theology (STD) from the Angelicum University in Rome and was a professor there for six years. He has taught at several colleges and seminaries in the United States. He is currently a mission preacher and retreat master for the Western Dominican Province. He also teaches two months of the year at Holy Apostles Seminary in Cromwell, Connecticut. Fr. Mullady has had fourteen series on the EWTN Global Catholic Network. He is the author of four books and numerous articles and writes the answer column in *Homiletic and Pastoral Review*. He is also designated as an official Missionary of Mercy by Pope Francis.